Collins

Junior Thesaurus

Emily Da Silva
Gouveia
Isabel Da Silva
Gouveia

Collins Junior Thesaurus

First published 2004

© HarperCollins*Publishers* Ltd 2004

10 9 8 7 6 5 4 3 2 1

ISBN 0 00 715428 3

A catalogue record for this book is available from the British Library.

Published by Collins
A division of HarperCollins*Publishers* Ltd
77–85 Fulham Palace Road
Hammersmith
London W6 8JB

www.collinseducation.com
Collins' complete catalogue and ordering
facility – only a click away!

www.harpercollins.co.uk
Visit the book lover's website

Compiler	Evelyn Goldsmith
Literacy consultant	Kay Hiatt, Rosemary Boys
Cover designer	Susi Martin
Design	Sylvia Tate, Perry Tate Design
Editor	Penny Smith
Indexer	Lyn Nesbitt-Smith of Indexing Specialists (UK) Ltd
Project Editors	Shannon Park, Lee Newman, Emma Thomas
Proofreader	Ian Brooke
Illustrators	Beccy Blake, Andrew Midgely, Lisa Smith of Sylvie Poggio Artist Agency, Sarah Warburton of Sylvie Poggio Artist Agency

Acknowledgements
The publishers would like to thank all the teachers, staff and pupils who contributed to this book:

Teacher advisors

Jill Burton	Sarah McKissock
Ruth Grainger	Maggie McLaren
Krys Hill	Amanda Sullivan
Lawrence Keel	

Schools
Hobbayne Primary School
Lena Gardens Primary School
Old Oak Primary School
Standens Barn Primary School
St Gregory's RC Primary School
Vicar's Green Primary School

Printed in Hong Kong by Printing Express Ltd, Hong Kong

Contents

Using this thesaurus

A thesaurus helps you choose exactly the right word to make your writing more interesting. In your writing, do you find you use words like **good, bad** and **nice** too often? A thesaurus will help you find other words with the same meaning.

How to find a word

You want to find a different way of saying **hungry**. What letter does it begin with? Use the alphabet line at the side of the page. The green box tells you that the words on this page start with **h**.

Think about the second letter of the word. You are looking for a word beginning with **hu**. Use the guide word at the top of the page. The guide word at the top left tells you the *first word* on that page. The guide word at the top right tells you the *last word* on that page. The guide word for this page is **hot** – it starts with **ho**. Does **hu** come after **ho**?

When you think you have the right page, look at the blue words. These are called headwords. The headwords are in alphabetical order. If you run your finger down the headwords on this page, you will see more than one word beginning with **hu**.

Once you have found the word **hungry**, you can choose the synonym.

guide word ······

① headword ─────

alphabet line ······

⑤ synonym ─────

⑨ antonym ─────

② numbered headword

③ part of speech

⑥ example sentence

④ definition

⑦ illustration

⑧ phrase

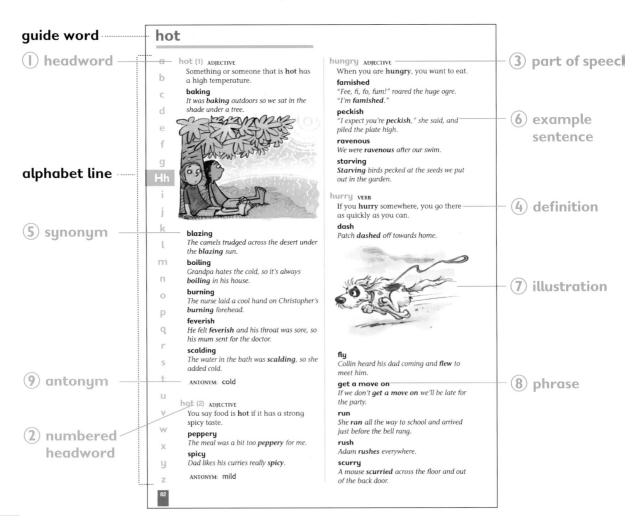

hot (1) ADJECTIVE
Something or someone that is **hot** has a high temperature.
baking
It was baking outdoors so we sat in the shade under a tree.

blazing
The camels trudged across the desert under the blazing sun.
boiling
Grandpa hates the cold, so it's always boiling in his house.
burning
The nurse laid a cool hand on Christopher's burning forehead.
feverish
He felt feverish and his throat was sore, so his mum sent for the doctor.
scalding
The water in the bath was scalding, so she added cold.
ANTONYM: cold

hot (2) ADJECTIVE
You say food is **hot** if it has a strong spicy taste.
peppery
The meal was a bit too peppery for me.
spicy
Dad likes his curries really spicy.
ANTONYM: mild

hungry ADJECTIVE
When you are **hungry**, you want to eat.
famished
"Fee, fi, fo, fum!" roared the huge ogre. "I'm famished."
peckish
"I expect you're peckish," she said, and piled the plate high.
ravenous
We were ravenous after our swim.
starving
Starving birds pecked at the seeds we put out in the garden.

hurry VERB
If you **hurry** somewhere, you go there as quickly as you can.
dash
Patch dashed off towards home.

fly
Collin heard his dad coming and flew to meet him.
get a move on
If we don't get a move on we'll be late for the party.
run
She ran all the way to school and arrived just before the bell rang.
rush
Adam rushes everywhere.
scurry
A mouse scurried across the floor and out of the back door.

82

4

Choosing the right synonym

(1) The headword is the word that you want to find a synonym for.

(2) On the same line as the headword, you will see a number in brackets. This tells you that this headword can have different meanings.

(3) Next you will see the part of speech. This tells you what type of word the headword is, such as a noun, verb, adjective, adverb or pronoun. If the word you want to find is a verb, make sure the headword you look at is also a verb.

(4) Underneath the headword, you will find the definition. The definition tells you what the headword means.

(5) The synonyms are listed below the definition of each headword. Synonyms have similar meanings to the headword.

(6) Every synonym in the *Collins Junior Thesaurus* has an example sentence. This shows you how the word might be used in speech or writing.

(7) Some synonyms have an illustration to help you read the word and understand its meaning.

(8) Some of the synonyms provided in this thesaurus are phrases, for example **get a move on**. The example sentence will help you see how to use this phrase in your writing.

(9) An antonym is a word that means the opposite of another. When a headword has an antonym, the antonym is shown at the end of the entry.

Other features of this thesaurus

This arrow → points to a booster. Boosters are lively words and phrases that can be used to replace a headword. Boosters are usually words that are used in speech as slang, in proverbs and in mottos. For example:

noisy ADJECTIVE
Someone or something **noisy** makes loud or unpleasant sounds.

boisterous
*Dad complained the party was getting far too **boisterous**.*

deafening
*Suddenly there was a **deafening** clap of thunder.*

loud
*The boys' game was much too **loud**.*

piercing
*She was a nice girl, but they couldn't stand her **piercing** laugh.*

→ ear-splitting

Picture pages and sections

There are special themed pages and sections throughout this thesaurus to support your writing.

Picture pages and **sections** have labelled illustrations and lists of things such as parts of the body, colours and different types of animal. The picture pages and sections listed on the **Contents** page.

Using the index

Using the index

The index lists all the synonyms and headwords in the thesaurus in alphabetical order. You can use it to look up any word in the thesaurus and find other synonyms.

How to find a synonym

You have written this sentence:

This is a genuine report so all the facts are genuine.

You want to find a different way of saying **genuine**, which is a synonym in the thesaurus.

First, find the word **genuine** in the index. What letter does it begin with? Flick through the index until you reach the section beginning with **Gg**.

Think about the second and third letters of the word. All the synonyms in the index are in alphabetical order. Run your finger down the list. You will find more than one word beginning with **gen**.

Keep looking until you find the word **genuine**.

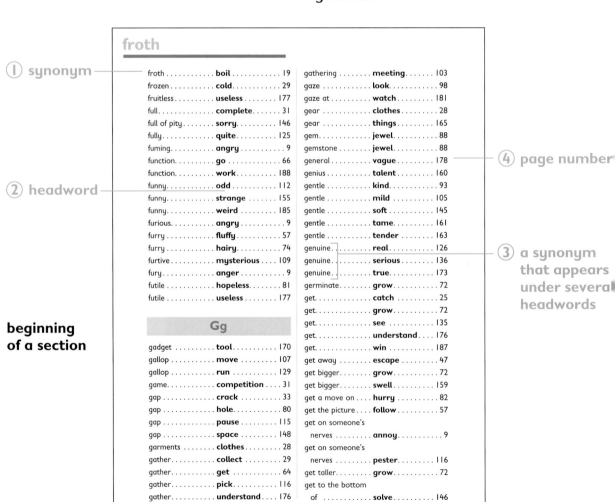

① synonym

② headword

beginning of a section

④ page number

③ a synonym that appears under several headwords

Looking up the synonym in the thesaurus

① Find the synonym. The synonym is the word or phrase in the first column.

② Find the headword. The headword is in the column next to the synonym.

③ The synonym **genuine** appears under several headwords, for example, **real**, **serious** and **true**. If you are sure which meaning of **genuine** you want to use, choose the right headword. If you are not sure, look up the headwords and check the definitions. In this case, you want to use the headword **true**.

④ Find the page number. The page on which you will find the headword is in the next column.

Choosing the right synonym

● Use the page number to find the page your synonym appears on.

● Find the headword you selected in the index.

● Look for the synonym that suits your writing.

● Use the example sentences to understand how each synonym can be used.

Now you can replace **genuine** in your sentence:

This is an accurate report so all the facts are genuine.

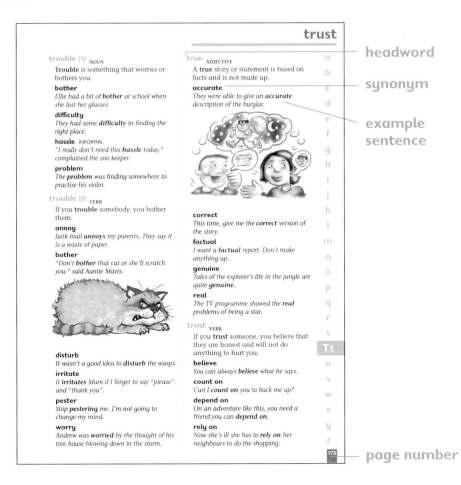

trust — headword

trouble (1) NOUN
Trouble is something that worries or bothers you.
bother
Ellie had a bit of bother at school when she lost her glasses.
difficulty
They had some difficulty in finding the right place.
hassle INFORMAL
"I really don't need this hassle today," complained the zoo keeper.
problem
The problem was finding somewhere to practise his violin.

trouble (2) VERB
If you trouble somebody, you bother them.
annoy
Junk mail annoys my parents. They say it is a waste of paper.
bother
"Don't bother that cat or she'll scratch you." said Auntie Mavis.

disturb
It wasn't a good idea to disturb the wasps.
irritate
It irritates Mum if I forget to say "please" and "thank you".
pester
Stop pestering me. I'm not going to change my mind.
worry
Andrew was worried by the thought of his tree house blowing down in the storm.

true ADJECTIVE — synonym
A **true** story or statement is based on facts and is not made up.
accurate — example sentence
They were able to give an accurate description of the burglar.
correct
This time, give me the correct version of the story.
factual
I want a factual report. Don't make anything up.
genuine
Tales of the explorer's life in the jungle are quite genuine.
real
The TV programme showed the real problems of being a star.

trust VERB
If you trust someone, you believe that they are honest and will not do anything to hurt you.
believe
You can always believe what he says.
count on
Can I count on you to back me up?
depend on
On an adventure like this, you need a friend you can depend on.
rely on
Now she's ill she has to rely on her neighbours to do the shopping.

a b c d e f g h i j k l m n o p q r s **Tt** u v w x y z

173 — page number

Aa

accident (1)   NOUN

An **accident** is something nasty that happens by chance.

calamity
*The flooding river caused a **calamity** and the house was wrecked.*

catastrophe
*That plane crash was a **catastrophe**.*

collision
*Mark damaged his bike in a **collision** with the gatepost.*

crash
*There was a bad **crash** on the motorway.*

disaster
*Tom's walk ended with a **disaster** when he fell in the canal.*

mishap
*"Just a **mishap**," said Dad, after his keys fell down the drain.*

accident (2)   NOUN

If something happens by **accident**, it was not planned.

chance
*The friends met by **chance** at the disco.*

coincidence
*Ben and Rosie got the same answers by **coincidence**.*

afraid   ADJECTIVE

Someone who is **afraid** thinks that something nasty might happen.

anxious
*Mole felt **anxious** in the wild wood.*

nervous
*"You don't need to be **nervous**," said the dentist. "This won't hurt a bit."*

panic-stricken
*They were **panic-stricken** when they heard the ice crack.*

petrified
*Emma was **petrified** during her ride on the big dipper.*

scared
*Goldilocks was **scared** when the three bears found her.*

worried
*Our cat was **worried** when the pet-shop owner picked up her kittens.*

→ numb with fear; scared to death

amphibian   NOUN

An **amphibian** is an animal that can live on land and in water.

TYPES OF AMPHIBIANS:

frog

newt

toad

anger NOUN

Anger is the strong feeling you have about something that is unfair.

fury
My little brother stamped his foot in fury when I wouldn't play with him.

outrage
There was outrage among farmers when the plans were announced.

rage
Nobody dared annoy the ogre, because his rage was terrible to see.

angry ADJECTIVE

If you feel **angry**, you are very cross.

annoyed
Alice was annoyed with the Mad Hatter and the March Hare.

cross
Steven was cross when his sister finished his jigsaw.

enraged
Michael was enraged when thieves stole his new bike.

furious
The old man was furious about the broken window.

infuriated
Grandpa was infuriated because squirrels had dug up his flower bulbs.

mad
I made my best friend mad by shouting at her.

wild
Sarah was really wild when her little brother scribbled on her work.

➔ climbing the walls; fuming; going ballistic; livid

ANTONYM: **pleased**

animal NOUN

Animals are living things that are not plants. Humans, mammals, birds, fish, reptiles and insects are all animals.

beast
Fabulous beasts roamed wild in the enchanted forest.

creature
Mice are timid creatures.

KINDS OF ANIMALS:

amphibian	fish	mammal
bird	insect	reptile

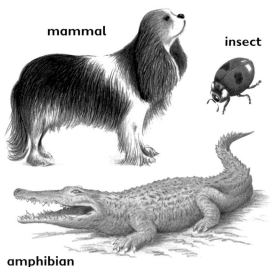

mammal

insect

amphibian

annoy VERB

If you do something that **annoys** someone, you make them cross.

bother
The horse lashed its tail at flies that were bothering it.

hassle INFORMAL
Stop hassling me or we won't go at all.

irritate
It irritates Thomas when people treat him like a child.

pester
The cubs would not stop pestering the old lion.

➔ drive someone crazy; get on someone' nerves

Aa

appear (1) VERB

If something **appears**, it moves into a place where you can see it.

come into view
At last the train came into view round the bend.

emerge
A mouse emerged from a small hole in the skirting board.

turn up
They waited ages for the bus to turn up.

appear (2) VERB

If someone **appears** in a show or play, they take part in it.

act
Our drama teacher is looking for people to act in Peter Pan.

perform
I've been asked to perform in the school concert tonight.

argument NOUN

An **argument** is a talk between people who do not agree.

disagreement
There was a disagreement about the new kitten's name.

fight
We had a bit of a fight over whose turn it was to wash up.

quarrel
Sophie was unhappy after the quarrel with her friend.

squabble
"I don't want the usual squabble about this," said Mum.

arrange (1) VERB

If you **arrange** something like a party, you make plans and organize it.

fix
We'd better fix the date soon or there won't be any seats left.

organize
My mum's great at organizing things, but she won't do any cooking.

plan
William's sister is planning a wedding at the end of the year.

arrange (2) VERB

If you **arrange** things like flowers, you group them in a special way.

group
Harry grouped the rocks according to size.

set out
The books were set out on the shelves.

sort
Dad sorted his files in alphabetical order to make them easy to find.

arrive VERB

When you **arrive** at a place, you reach it at the end of your journey.

come
What time's Jeremy coming?

turn up
Chloe could turn up any minute now.

ask (1) VERB

You **ask** for something when you want to be given it.

beg
*James **begged** his dad for a mountain bike for his birthday.*

demand
*"Who's been playing with my camera?" **demanded** Dad.*

order
*The highwayman **ordered** them to hand over their jewels.*

plead
*Holly **pleaded** to be allowed to stay up late and read her book.*

request
*The sign read, "Parents are **requested** to control their children."*

ask (2) VERB

If you **ask** someone a question, you are trying to find something out.

enquire
*"May I **enquire**," said the teacher, "why that mouse is in your pocket?"*

find out
*I'll **find out** what time the train goes from the station.*

interrogate
*"You don't have to **interrogate** me," said Nina. "I'll tell you anyway."*

question
*The police said they were **questioning** a number of people.*

ask (3) VERB

If you **ask** someone somewhere, you want them to come.

invite
*I **invited** all my friends to my birthday party at the pool.*

summon
*Christopher was **summoned** to the head teacher's office.*

attractive ADJECTIVE

If someone or something is **attractive**, they are nice to look at.

beautiful
*The car stopped and a **beautiful** woman got out.*

charming
*We had tea in the garden of a **charming** little cottage.*

handsome
*"I'll turn into a **handsome** prince if you kiss me," said the frog.*

lovely
*There was a **lovely** view from the window.*

pretty
*On the way, we passed through several **pretty** villages.*

awful ADJECTIVE

Something **awful** is very unpleasant or bad.

bad
*The weather was so **bad** we had to cancel the picnic.*

dreadful
*Sarah had a **dreadful** cold and found it hard to breathe.*

horrible
*A **horrible** smell came wafting from the witch's cauldron.*

terrible
*Rosetta's writing is so **terrible** nobody can read it.*

unpleasant
*They've painted the walls an **unpleasant** shade of green.*

Aa
b
c
d
e
f
g
h
i
j
k
l
m
n
o
p
q
r
s
t
u
v
w
x
y
z

Bb

bad (1) ADJECTIVE

You say somebody is **bad** if they are naughty or wicked.

criminal
The police arrested four of the men for **criminal** behaviour.

disobedient
I have a very **disobedient** dog. He doesn't come when I call him.

evil
Stories often tell of the fight between good and **evil** forces.

vile
"You're **vile**!" she screamed. "Go away!"

wicked
The **wicked** queen gave Snow White a poisoned apple.

ANTONYM: good

bad (2) ADJECTIVE

If something is **bad**, it is harmful, unpleasant or upsetting.

appalling
Conditions on the road were **appalling**. There were several accidents.

disgusting
A **disgusting** smell came from the cave. An ogre was washing his underpants.

dreadful
The kitchen was in a **dreadful** state when Sanjay had finished making a cake.

harmful
Pollution is **harmful** for the environment.

hazardous
There is thick fog on the motorway and driving conditions are **hazardous**.

horrid
Amy stood in the doorway. "I've just had a **horrid** dream," she said.

nasty
The medicine tasted really **nasty**.

severe
Darren the dragon had a **severe** coughing fit and set light to the furniture.

terrible
The weathermen were forecasting **terrible** floods for the weekend.

unpleasant
Walking to school was really **unpleasant**. Slush was everywhere.

bad (3) ADJECTIVE

You say something is **bad** if it is of poor quality.

careless
Your answers are right, but your presentation is **careless**.

faulty
Robert's handling of the cricket bat was **faulty** so he couldn't hit the ball.

poor
The lighting was so **poor** nobody could see the steps properly.

shoddy
The cupboard was so **shoddy** that it fell apart when I opened it.

wrong
The instructions were **wrong** so we couldn't see how to assemble the kit.

ban VERB

If someone **bans** something, you are not allowed to do it.

forbid

*Our teacher has **forbidden** sweets and crisps in the classroom.*

prohibit

*The council has **prohibited** skateboarding in the shopping centre.*

band (1) NOUN

A **band** is a small number of people, like a group of musicians.

group

*Five of us have formed a pop **group**.*

orchestra

*Our school has its own **orchestra**.*

band (2) NOUN

A **band** can be a strip of material such as iron, cloth or rubber.

hoop

*Metal **hoops** held the barrel together.*

strap

*Strong **straps** keep the luggage safe on the roof rack.*

strip

***Strips** of gold round the sailor's sleeve showed he was in charge.*

bang NOUN

A **bang** is a sudden loud noise.

blast

*They heard a **blast** from the rocket as it launched.*

boom

*A **boom** from the explosive echoed round the quarry.*

explosion

*There was a deafening **explosion** and the ground shook.*

knock

*Suddenly, there was a loud **knock** at the front door.*

bare (1) ADJECTIVE

If something is **bare**, it has nothing in it or on it.

empty

*She looked for food in the cupboard, but it was **empty**.*

unfurnished

*The place was **unfurnished** except for a table and one chair.*

bare (2) ADJECTIVE

If part of your body is **bare**, it is not covered by clothes.

naked

*The baby lay **naked**, kicking her legs.*

nude

*The painting showed a **nude** woman holding a towel.*

undressed

*"You can't come in!" she shrieked. "I'm **undressed**!"*

basic ADJECTIVE

Basic means the simplest things you need, or need to know.

chief

*The **chief** thing to remember when hiking is to shut gates behind you.*

essential

*Water is an **essential** requirement for all living creatures.*

important

*An **important** rule is to check the traffic before you cross a road.*

main

*The **main** thing is not to panic if the fire alarm goes off.*

standard

*Our car is a **standard** model.*

a
Bb
c
d
e
f
g
h
i
j
k
l
m
n
o
p
q
r
s
t
u
v
w
x
y
z

beautiful

beautiful (1) ADJECTIVE
You say something is **beautiful** if it gives you great pleasure to look at or listen to.

amazing
There's an **amazing** view of the countryside from here.

attractive
It's an **attractive** village with a very old church in the centre.

enchanting
The castle has an **enchanting** garden.

fine
It was a **fine** day so we had a picnic on the beach.

glorious
"Summer weather here is absolutely **glorious**," exclaimed Gran.

gorgeous
Princess Jane wore a **gorgeous** dress sparkling with jewels.

graceful
The ballerina performed a **graceful** curtsey for the audience.

incredible
It was an **incredible** building with dozens of turrets.

magnificent
The king wore **magnificent** robes.

pretty
There's a **pretty** cottage round the corner.

spectacular
The fireworks were **spectacular**.

splendid
The singer had a **splendid** voice.

stunning
"Wow! Your new hairstyle is absolutely **stunning**!" said Fiona.

beautiful (2) ADJECTIVE
You say someone is **beautiful** if they are lovely to look at.

good
Mum looked really **good** in her new outfit.

good-looking
The girl next door's really **good-looking**.

lovely
The princess looked **lovely** on her wedding day.

believe VERB

If you **believe** someone or something, you think what is said is true.

accept
*She can't **accept** that she is wrong.*

trust
*I **trusted** him, but it seems he was not telling the truth.*

bend (1) VERB

When something **bends**, it becomes curved or crooked.

buckle
*Her bike hit a rock that badly **buckled** the front wheel.*

fold
*The blacksmith heated a strip of iron and **folded** it in half.*

twist
*A man **twisted** long balloons into the shape of an animal.*

bend (2) NOUN

A **bend** is a curve in something.

corner
*The house you are looking for is round the next **corner**.*

curve
*Round a **curve** in the river was the waterfall where we ate our picnic.*

loop
***Loops** in the mountain road made the drive scary.*

bend (3) VERB

When you **bend**, you move your body forwards and downwards.

bow
*The farmer **bowed** his back under a heavy sack of oats.*

crouch
*We **crouched** down out of sight.*

lean
*Sam **leaned** over and stroked the kitten.*

stoop
***Stooping** down, she touched the track made by the deer.*

better (1) ADJECTIVE

Something that is **better** than something else is of a higher standard or quality.

finer
*I couldn't have had a **finer** teacher.*

greater
*After all his study, he had a **greater** understanding of the subject.*

better (2) ADJECTIVE

If you are feeling **better** after an illness, you are not feeling so ill.

healthier
*Sean certainly looks much **healthier** now.*

recovering
*Grandma had a nasty fall but she is now **recovering**.*

stronger
*I felt really weak, but I'm getting **stronger** every day.*

big

big (1) ADJECTIVE

Something or somebody **big** is large in size.

bulky
The parcel was too **bulky** to fit through the letterbox.

enormous
Lionel got squashed when an **enormous** dog sat on him.

giant
At the end of the party Uncle Simon set off a **giant** firework.

grand
The concert was in a very **grand** house.

great
There was a **great** gasp from the audience.

huge
A **huge** tree blocked their path.

immense
This money will be an **immense** help to the new hospital.

large
Matt took a **large** bite of chocolate cake and grinned contentedly.

massive
A **massive** rock crashed to the ground in front of them.

mighty
There was a **mighty** roar from the crowd when we scored the winning goal.

vast
A **vast** mountain rose before them, its top lost in mist.

→ colossal; gigantic; mammoth

big (2) ADJECTIVE

Sometimes **big** can mean important, or having a lot of influence.

important
"Hey, I think we've found something **important**," said Carter.

serious
Burglary is a **serious** problem in this area.

bin VERB

If you **bin** something, you throw it away.

discard
Mum tried to persuade Dad to **discard** his old jacket.

scrap
She decided to **scrap** everything she'd written so far.

bind VERB

If you **bind** something, you tie something like string or cloth tightly round it so that it is held in place.

attach
In our first-aid class, we were taught to **attach** splints to a damaged limb.

fasten
The woodcutter always **fastens** the firewood with twine.

join
Simon used extra-strong tape to **join** the broken struts together.

tie
"I'll **tie** a handkerchief round your leg to stop the bleeding," said Mum.

bird NOUN

A **bird** is an animal with two legs, two wings and feathers.

PET BIRDS:
budgerigar
cockatiel

budgerigar

FARM BIRDS:
chicken   goose
duck   turkey

duck

BRITISH GARDEN BIRDS:
blackbird
blue tit
chaffinch
robin
sparrow
thrush
wren

robin

BIRDS OF PREY:
buzzard
eagle
falcon
kestrel
owl

kestrel

BIRDS THAT LIVE NEAR WATER:
coot   moorhen
curlew   pelican
duck   penguin
flamingo   puffin
goose   stork
gull   swan
kingfisher

kingfisher

OTHER BIRDS:
emu
kiwi
kookaburra
ostrich
parrot
peacock
vulture

peacock

bit NOUN

A **bit** of something is a small piece of it.

chip
We found a chip of Roman pottery in the garden.

chunk
Henry broke off a chunk of chocolate.

crumb
Under the table, birds were pecking at leftover crumbs.

fragment
They were looking for fossils but found only a small fragment of bone.

morsel
Oliver was so hungry he ate up every last morsel of pie.

part
Julia liked the part in the film where owls brought messages.

piece
She couldn't finish the jigsaw. There was one piece missing.

portion
Every guest had a portion of cheese.

scrap
There was an interesting scrap of paper at the crime scene.

shred
The kitten tore the curtains to shreds.

slab
A slab of white stone covered the mouth of the tomb.

speck
If there was a speck of dust my mum would find it.

body

body NOUN
Your **body** is every
part of you.

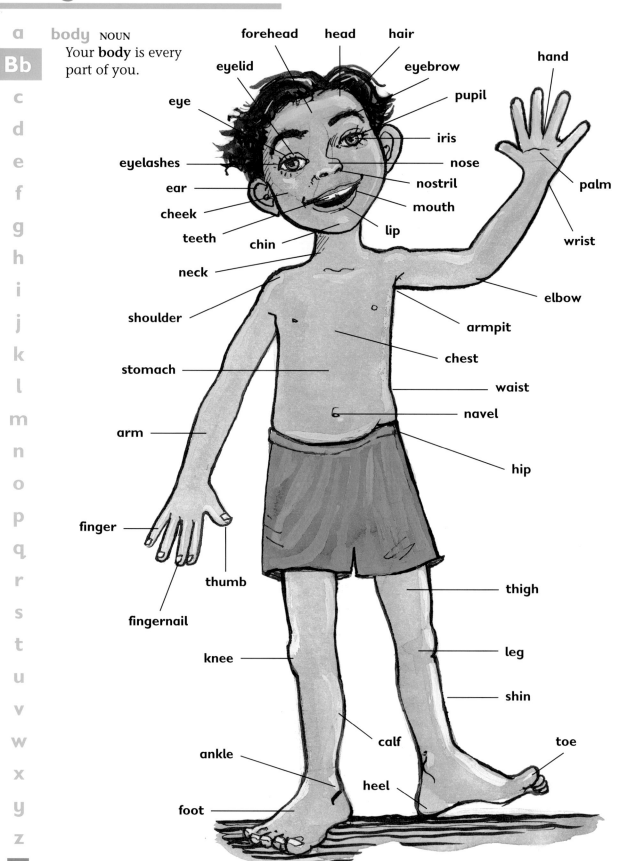

forehead
head
hair
eyelid
eyebrow
hand
eye
pupil
iris
eyelashes
nose
ear
nostril
palm
cheek
mouth
teeth
lip
wrist
chin
neck
elbow
shoulder
armpit
chest
stomach
waist
navel
arm
hip
finger
thumb
thigh
fingernail
leg
knee
shin
calf
toe
ankle
heel
foot

boil VERB

When liquid **boils**, it bubbles.

bubble

Stew **bubbled** furiously on the stove.

foam

Warm the butter until it **foams**.

froth

Hot milk rose in the pan and **frothed** over the top.

heat

Heat the mixture for five minutes.

book NOUN

A **book** is a number of pages held together inside a cover.

KINDS OF BOOKS:

album	manual
atlas	notebook
diary	novel
dictionary	storybook
encyclopedia	textbook
jotter	thesaurus

boring ADJECTIVE

Something **boring** is so dull that you have no interest in it.

dreary

We spent a **dreary** afternoon queuing for concert tickets.

dull

The film was so **dull** that William fell asleep in the middle of it.

monotonous

The television presenter droned on in a **monotonous** voice.

→ mind-numbing

ANTONYM: exciting

bottom (1) NOUN

The **bottom** of something is the lowest part of it.

base

There were lots of fallen rocks at the **base** of the cliff.

bed

The **bed** of the river was sandy.

foot

They stopped at the **foot** of the mountain and looked up.

foundation

It was an old pillar. The **foundation** was crumbling.

bottom (2) NOUN

Your **bottom** is the part of your body that you sit on.

behind

Llewelyn sat there so long that his **behind** went numb.

bum INFORMAL

"Does my **bum** look big in this?" Abdul's teenage sister asked.

buttocks

A fall on the ice bruised his **buttocks**.

rear

While Tom was looking round the farm, a goat butted him in the **rear**.

box

box NOUN

A **box** is a container with straight sides, made from something stiff, like cardboard, wood or plastic.

carton
*They took a **carton** of strawberries with them on the picnic.*

case
*When we moved, all our books were packed in **cases**.*

chest
*Tommy keeps his toys in a **chest**.*

packet
*Sarah wanted her own small **packet** of cereal for breakfast.*

brave ADJECTIVE

If you are **brave**, you show you can do something even if it is frightening.

adventurous
*Alice was **adventurous** and liked to try new things.*

bold
*The kitten was **bold** enough to tap the dog on its nose.*

courageous
*The **courageous** dentist agreed to check the lion's teeth.*

daring
*King Arthur's knights did all sorts of **daring** deeds.*

fearless
*People doing extreme sports seem **fearless**.*

→ heroic; intrepid

ANTONYM: **cowardly**

break (1) VERB

If you **break** something, it splits into pieces or stops working.

chip
*"Don't bang that plate down or you'll **chip** it," said Mum.*

crack
*The ogre gazed at his reflection. This made the mirror **crack**.*

crumble
*She sat anxiously **crumbling** a piece of bread in her fingers.*

fall apart
*Jeremy gloomily watched his bookshelves **fall apart**.*

shatter
*Her voice is so loud it could **shatter** glass.*

smash
*The guard saw the priceless statue **smash** on the ground.*

snap
*Simone heard a twig **snap** behind her. She spun round in alarm.*

splinter
*The Snow Queen made the glass **splinter** into a thousand fragments.*

break (2) NOUN

A **break** is a short rest or change.

interval
*In the play there's a short **interval** between two acts.*

pause
*There was a **pause** while the teacher hunted for her notes.*

rest
*"I'm exhausted," said Daniel. "Let's have a **rest** before we go out."*

bright (1) ADJECTIVE

Someone who is **bright** is quick at learning or noticing things.

brainy
*My brother's really **brainy**. He wants to go to university.*

clever
*"If you're **clever**, you'll put the watch together again," said Jessie.*

intelligent
*Guide dogs have to be very **intelligent**.*

sharp
*"You're very **sharp**," said the old lady, "but you still haven't solved the puzzle."*

smart
*Some people think squirrels are **smart**, but they often can't find nuts they've buried.*

bright (2) ADJECTIVE

Bright lights and colours are strong and startling.

brilliant
*Parrots' **brilliant** colours make them easy to see.*

colourful
*The magician produced a **colourful** string of knotted scarves.*

dazzling
*They shaded their eyes against his **dazzling** white shirt.*

glaring
***Glaring** headlights blinded Dad and he had to stop the car.*

glowing
*The bonfire was **glowing** in the dark.*

bright (3) ADJECTIVE

Someone who is **bright** is cheerful and lively.

cheerful
*I like Alex. He's always so **cheerful** and jolly in class.*

lively
*Kamal felt **lively** and refreshed when he woke up.*

bring VERB

If you **bring** something or someone, you have them with you when you arrive.

carry
*He arrived **carrying** presents for everyone.*

guide
*You'll need someone to **guide** you back if it's dark.*

lead
*Firemen often have to **lead** people out of burning buildings.*

take
*Taxis were used to **take** guests to the wedding reception.*

build VERB

If you **build** something, you make it by joining things together.

create
*Dad **created** a wonderful tree house for us.*

make
*The children **made** an igloo with small blocks of snow.*

put up
*We **put up** a fence round the guinea pigs to keep them safe.*

building

building NOUN

A **building** is a place, such as a house, that has walls and a roof.

BUILDINGS TO LIVE IN:

apartment   detached house
bungalow   flat
castle   semi-detached house
cottage   terraced house

castle

terraced houses

cottage

BUILDINGS TO WORK IN:

factory
fire station
garage
hospital
laboratory
library
lighthouse
police station
shop
skyscraper
studio
windmill

windmill

skyscraper

lighthouse

BUILDINGS TO WORSHIP IN:

cathedral
chapel
church
mosque
synagogue
temple

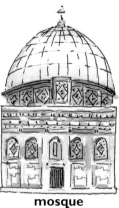
mosque

cathedral

temple

bully VERB

Someone who **bullies** people hurts or frightens them.

frighten
The witch **frightened** him into helping her gather mushrooms.

threaten
One of the big boys **threatened** us.

torment
Stop **tormenting** your little sister.

bump NOUN

A **bump** is a raised, uneven part on a surface.

bulge
A bag of sweets made a **bulge** in his jacket pocket.

hump
There are **humps** here to slow down traffic.

lump
Our old mattress is full of **lumps**.

swelling
Chloe had a nasty **swelling** on her finger.

bump into VERB

If you **bump into** something, you hit it while you are moving.

bang into
The brakes on his bike failed and he **banged into** the fence.

collide with
In the dark our car **collided with** a tree.

hit
He ran into the road without looking and **hit** a cyclist.

strike
She **struck** a litterbin when she lost control of her skateboard.

bunch NOUN

A **bunch** is a group of things together, like flowers or grapes.

bouquet
The bride carried a **bouquet** of roses.

posy
Emma gave her mum a lovely **posy** of bright flowers.

spray
Sprays of holly brightened the hall.

bundle NOUN

A **bundle** is a number of small things gathered together.

batch
The first **batch** of letters arrived next day.

collection
We put a **collection** of newspapers out for recycling.

heap
On the table was a **heap** of clothes for the charity shop.

pile
A **pile** of dirty washing was waiting to go to the launderette.

burn VERB

If something is **burning**, it is on fire.

blaze
A bonfire **blazed** in the garden.

flame
The fire began to **flame** green as it caught the ink.

flare
Suddenly a match **flared** in the darkness.

flicker
He blew gently on the spark and the fire began to **flicker**.

burst VERB

When something like a balloon or tyre **bursts**, it splits apart suddenly.

explode
One of the bottles **exploded** in the heat.

pop
The baby laughed with delight when the bubbles **popped**.

puncture
A nail **punctured** one of my tyres.

a
Bb
c
d
e
f
g
h
i
j
k
l
m
n
o
p
q
r
s
t
u
v
w
x
y
z

Cc

call (1) VERB
If you **call**, you phone or visit someone.

phone
*I'll **phone** you as soon as I get there.*

ring
*Give me a **ring** one day next week.*

visit
*Grandpa wants us to **visit** tomorrow.*

call (2) VERB
If you **call** someone, you shout for them.

cry
*"Where are you hiding?" she **cried**.*

cry out
*Rashid **cried out** in delight when he saw the otter.*

shout
*"Come on Ben. You'll be late for school," Mum **shouted**.*

yell
*"Come on in!" Tracy **yelled**. "The water is great!"*

calm (1) ADJECTIVE
If something is **calm**, it is still and peaceful.

peaceful
*Everything seemed **peaceful** in the church.*

still
*That afternoon the breeze had dropped and the air was **still**.*

calm (2) ADJECTIVE
If you are **calm**, you do not seem worried or excited.

cool
*She was surprisingly **cool** about the exciting news.*

quiet
*The children were very **quiet** until they saw the mouse.*

car NOUN
A **car** is a road vehicle with wheels and an engine. It needs a driver and usually has room for passengers.

KINDS OF CARS:

convertible	people carrier
estate	racing car
four-wheel drive	saloon
hatchback	sports car
limousine	taxi
minicab	vintage car

vintage car

care VERB
If you **care** about something, you are concerned about it.

be bothered
*I **am bothered** about missing my swimming lessons.*

be concerned
*My brother **is concerned** about the world's endangered wildlife.*

mind
*Gavin said he didn't **mind** who won the game of chess.*

careful (1) ADJECTIVE

If you are **careful**, you try to do things well.

accurate
*The soldier had to be **accurate**. He had only one chance to hit the target.*

thorough
*We made a **thorough** search of the room.*

careful (2) ADJECTIVE

If you are **careful**, you try to do things safely.

alert
*In Australia there is a danger of bush fires, and people have to be **alert**.*

cautious
*The lifeguard taught them to be **cautious** around the pool.*

wary
*Joe knew he had to be **wary** of strangers.*

watchful
*With a toddler, you have to be **watchful** all the time.*

careless (1) ADJECTIVE

If you are **careless**, you do not take enough care.

messy
*My little sister is a **messy** eater.*

sloppy
*Her knitting was **sloppy**, with dropped stitches everywhere.*

untidy
*The professor was **untidy**. Now he couldn't find his papers.*

careless (2) ADJECTIVE

Careless can also mean not being sensible about things.

reckless
*Sam took a **reckless** leap over the river.*

thoughtless
*Only **thoughtless** people went out in the storm without a jacket.*

carry VERB

When you **carry** something, you pick it up and take it with you.

move
*He **moved** the plant over to the window.*

take
*We'd better **take** an umbrella.*

transport
*We need a van to **transport** our furniture.*

catch (1) VERB

If you catch something, like measles, you get that illness.

come down with
*"Stay away from me or you'll **come down with** chickenpox too," said Beth.*

get
*I don't want to **get** his cold.*

go down with
*It's just like Ross to **go down with** something at the wrong moment.*

catch (2) VERB

If you **catch** somebody or something, you capture them.

arrest
*The police want to **arrest** a man they suspect of burglary.*

capture
*Prison guards set a trap to **capture** the escaped prisoner.*

trap
*"**Trap** that spider," said Granny, "then put it outside."*

change

a b **Cc** d e f g h i j k l m n o p q r s t u v w x y z

change (1) VERB

When you **change** something, it becomes different.

alter
*The tailor said he could soon **alter** the length of the trouser legs.*

modify
*Let's **modify** the plan. We'll go this afternoon instead.*

reorganize
*"Oh no!" cried Mrs Jones. "I'm going to have to **reorganize** everything."*

revise
*The teacher said my story was good, but I should **revise** the ending.*

change (2) VERB

When something **changes**, it becomes different.

develop
*Tadpoles soon **develop** into frogs.*

shift
*The wind **shifted** to the west.*

turn
*Caterpillars **turn** into moths or butterflies.*

change (3) VERB

If you **change** something, you replace it with something else.

exchange
*"Can I **exchange** this blue shirt for a green one?" asked the customer.*

swap
*Henry wanted to **swap** his pop music CD for one of Rosie's.*

switch
*I didn't see him **switch** his old pen for my new one.*

chase VERB

If you **chase** someone, you try to catch them.

follow
*The boys **followed** the man they suspected of stealing a bike.*

hunt
*Our cat was out all night, **hunting** mice and rats.*

pursue
*Police **pursued** the speeding car for miles along the motorway.*

trail
*It was easy to **trail** the robber by following his footprints in the snow.*

check VERB

If you **check** something, you make sure it is correct and safe.

examine
*The witch frowned and **examined** the contents of the cauldron.*

inspect
*The mechanic **inspected** the car's brakes.*

make sure
*Before we set off, I **made sure** we'd remembered everything.*

test
*He **tested** the ground in case it was boggy.*

choose VERB

When you **choose**, you decide what to have or do.

elect
*They quickly **elected** a new leader.*

name
*Each one **named** the person they wanted.*

pick
*He **picked** the biggest cake he could find.*

select
*They were told to **select** a book and read for the rest of the lesson.*

take
*We **took** the shortest way.*

clean (1) VERB

If you **clean** something, you remove dirt from it.

DIFFERENT WAYS OF CLEANING:

bathe	scrub
brush	shampoo
dust	sponge
mop up	sweep
polish	vacuum
rinse	wash
scour	wipe

clean (2) ADJECTIVE

If something is **clean**, it is free from dirt.

blank
She took a **blank** sheet and began to write.

sparkling
Penelope polished the glasses until they were **sparkling**.

spotless
The floor was **spotless** by the time they'd finished mopping it.

clear (1) ADJECTIVE

If something you say or write is **clear**, it is easy to understand.

evident
It was **evident** she didn't like me.

obvious
It was **obvious** from the first sentence that this was a sad book.

plain
"I'll make my idea **plain**, in words of one syllable," his brother said.

simple
The instructions were really **simple** and easy to follow.

clear (2) ADJECTIVE

On a **clear** day there are no clouds in the sky.

bright
On a **bright** day there are strong shadows on the ground.

cloudless
After the storm the sun shone brightly in the **cloudless** sky.

fine
"If the weather's **fine** we'll go to the beach tomorrow," said Dad.

sunny
It was **sunny** one minute and raining heavily the next.

clear (3) ADJECTIVE

If a space is **clear**, there is nothing in it or it is free from things you don't want.

bare
The room was **bare** when we got it ready for decorating.

empty
For once, the car park was **empty** and Mum could park close to the shops.

clever

clever ADJECTIVE
Someone who is **clever** can learn and understand things easily.

brainy
Matt is really **brainy**. He gets top marks for everything.

bright
The baby's very **bright**. She's saying lots of words already.

crafty
A **crafty** old fox sneaked into the kitchen and stole the sausages.

cunning
She disguised her scar with a **cunning** use of make-up.

gifted
Kamal is a **gifted** writer.

intelligent
Our cat's quite **intelligent**. It understands ten words.

inventive
Matt was really **inventive** when it came to making up excuses.

sharp
That old man is still as **sharp** as ever.

skilful
Finches are **skilful** at getting the shells off sunflower seeds.

talented
He was a **talented** musician who could play any instrument well.

climb VERB
When you **climb** something, you move upwards.

ascend
The lift **ascended** so rapidly it took their breath away.

clamber
They **clambered** up the steep hill, clutching at bushes.

shin up
He **shinned up** a tree and looked through his telescope.

clothes PLURAL NOUN
Clothes are the things people wear, such as shirts, trousers and dresses.

clothing
You'll need warm **clothing** if you want to watch the fireworks.

costume
The actors in the film wore wonderful bright **costumes**.

dress
We were asked to wear informal **dress** to the dance.

garments
The charity shop is always glad of **garments** we no longer need.

gear
Sebastian had to have all the right **gear** for skateboarding.

outfit
Mum said her new **outfit** would be perfect for the wedding.

wardrobe
A famous designer planned the **wardrobe** for the musical.

wear
The shop sold everything you could want in the way of outdoor **wear**.

cold ADJECTIVE

If the weather is **cold**, the temperature outside is low.

WORDS THAT DESCRIBE THE COLD:

arctic	frozen
biting	icy
bitter	raw
chilly	wintry
cool	
freezing	
frosty	

collect VERB

If you **collect** a number of things, you bring them together.

assemble
*They **assembled** lots of food for the midnight feast.*

gather
*We went out to **gather** blackberries from a field near our house.*

hoard
*David **hoarded** empty glass bottles for his display.*

raise
*The school is trying to **raise** money for Children In Need.*

save
*We have been asked to **save** used stamps for a school project.*

collection NOUN

A **collection** is a group of things brought together over a period of time.

assortment
*The bathroom shelf is full of an **assortment** of shampoo bottles.*

heap
*Now and again, Dad adds another book to the **heap**.*

mass
*Dan worked his way through a **mass** of clothes to find his jeans.*

pile
*There was a **pile** of smelly old trainers in the corner.*

set
*"One more card and I'll have a complete **set**," said Raymond.*

colour

colour NOUN

The **colour** of something is the way it looks in daylight.

shade
*The walls were painted in different **shades**.*

tint
*The autumn leaves were taking on a warm red **tint**.*

DIFFERENT COLOURS:

black

blue
navy
sky blue
turquoise

brown
chocolate
coffee
fawn

green
bottle-green
lime

orange
tan

pink
rose

purple
lavender
lilac
mauve

red
crimson
scarlet
vermilion

white
cream
ivory

yellow
amber
gold

---

come VERB

To **come** to a place is to move there or arrive there.

appear
*We all giggled when the magician's rabbit **appeared** on stage.*

approach
*The guard dog growled loudly when the stranger **approached**.*

arrive
*The train **arrived**, and Grandma got out.*

draw near
*As they **drew near** to the castle, the great door opened.*

show up
*Most of the acts were good, but the conjuror didn't **show up**.*

turn up
*"Don't worry about us. We'll **turn up** later," said Ted.*

visit
*The Mayor is going to **visit** this afternoon.*

ANTONYM: go

comfortable (1) ADJECTIVE

Something **comfortable** makes you feel relaxed and snug.

cosy
*My room's warm and **cosy** in winter, even when it's freezing outside.*

snug
*Jamil felt **snug** tucked up in bed.*

soft
*Charlotte snuggled into the **soft** pillow and fell asleep straight away.*

comfortable (2) ADJECTIVE

If you are **comfortable**, you feel at ease.

contented
*The cat looked **contented** stretching out beside the fire.*

happy
*He was **happy** in his new room.*

relaxed
*Rebecca felt **relaxed** in the company of her friends.*

ANTONYM: uncomfortable

common ADJECTIVE

If something is **common**, you often see it or it often happens.

average
It's **average** behaviour for a boy of his age.

everyday
Children feeding ducks on the pond is an **everyday** sight in this park.

standard
Power steering is **standard** in many cars that are made today.

usual
It is quite **usual** to see dogs and cats getting on well together.

competition NOUN

A **competition** is an event to see who is best at doing something.

championship
Our school is taking part in the junior swimming **championship**.

contest
There was a fierce **contest** between the red and blue teams.

game
Supporters cheered when their team won the **game**.

race
Attilio was by far the fastest runner and easily won the **race**.

tournament
My brother is through to the finals of the table-tennis **tournament**.

complete (1) ADJECTIVE

If something is **complete**, there is nothing missing.

entire
I've got the **entire** set of famous people in my album.

full
The teacher wanted a **full** report of the science experiment.

whole
Amy recited the **whole** poem without a single mistake.

complete (2) VERB

If you **complete** something, you finish it.

conclude
The head teacher **concluded** his lecture with a warning about litter.

do
Have you **done** your homework?

end
Simon **ended** his talk by asking if there were any questions.

finish
Charles couldn't think how to **finish** his story.

conversation NOUN

If you have a **conversation** with someone, you talk to each other.

chat
My mum likes to have a **chat** with friends over a cup of coffee.

discussion
There was a long **discussion** about which class Sheena should be put in.

gossip
The opening of the new school provided plenty of **gossip**.

talk
"I think we should have a **talk** about this," said his teacher.

cook

cook VERB

When you **cook** food, you prepare it for eating by heating it.

WAYS OF COOKING:
bake
barbecue
boil
fry
grill
microwave
poach
roast
steam
stew
stir-fry
toast

copy (1) NOUN

A **copy** is something made to look like something else.

fake
*The police say that painting is a **fake**.*

forgery
*He thought the man gave him a twenty-pound note, but it was a **forgery**.*

imitation
*Those jewels are only **imitations**. They're made of glass.*

photocopy
*"Can you give me a **photocopy** of that page?" asked Domenica.*

print
*It's not an original painting. It's a **print**.*

replica
*Manuel bought a plastic **replica** of the Eiffel Tower.*

copy (2) VERB

If you **copy** what someone does, you do the same thing.

follow
*"You must **follow** my movements exactly," said the dance teacher.*

imitate
*She can **imitate** her mum's voice.*

impersonate
*Frank is really good at **impersonating** famous people.*

mimic
*Ben can **mimic** the sounds animals make.*

mirror
*We carefully **mirrored** the movements of the karate teacher.*

trace
*Kim carefully **traced** the outline of the country into her book.*

correct ADJECTIVE

Something that is **correct** is true and has no mistakes.

accurate
Make sure that your measurements are ***accurate***, *or the pieces will not fit together.*

exact
It's no good guessing the amount of flour you need, it must be ***exact***.

precise
"It's very important that the details you give are ***precise***," *said the policeman.*

right
In the test, all his answers were ***right***.

true
"Your report may be exciting," said her teacher, "but is it ***true***?"*

cosy ADJECTIVE

A house or room that is **cosy** is comfortable and warm and not too big.

comfortable
It was a ***comfortable*** *room with lots of deep armchairs and thick rugs.*

snug
We love our house because it's so ***snug***.

warm
The fire sent out a ***warm***, *welcoming glow.*

count VERB

If you **count** a number of things, you find out how many there are.

add up
She ***added up*** *her pocket money to see if there was enough to go to the cinema.*

calculate
Patrick ***calculated*** *the number of hours he had spent doing his homework.*

tally
The whole class stayed to ***tally*** *the votes for the football captain.*

work out
Work out *how much you've got, and how much more you need to buy this bike.*

cover VERB

If you **cover** something, you put something else over it to protect or hide it.

cloak
Mist ***cloaked*** *the mountain top, making it too dangerous to climb.*

conceal
The boy ***concealed*** *his work with his hand.*

hide
During winter a blanket of snow ***hid*** *the lawn and flowerbeds.*

mask
Edmund ***masked*** *his feeling of dismay with a smile.*

crack NOUN

A **crack** is a line or gap on something that shows it is damaged.

crevice
Many spiders lurked in ***crevices*** *in the old stone wall.*

gap
They had to watch the game through a ***gap*** *in the fence.*

split
One of the pieces of wood had a large ***split*** *at the end.*

crash NOUN

A **crash** is a sudden loud noise like something breaking.

clash
Fabian brought the cymbals together with a ***clash***.

clatter
The metal tray dropped to the ground with a ***clatter***.

smash
There was a ***smash*** *as the tea things hit the floor.*

crime NOUN

A **crime** is something that is against the law of a country.

KINDS OF CRIMES:

arson	mugging	smuggling
burglary	murder	stealing
graffiti	piracy	terrorism
hijacking	robbery	theft
joyriding	shoplifting	vandalism

criminal NOUN

A **criminal** is someone who has done something that is against the law.

KINDS OF CRIMINALS:

arsonist	murderer	terrorist
burglar	pirate	thief
graffitist	robber	vandal
hijacker	shoplifter	
joyrider	smuggler	
mugger		

crooked ADJECTIVE

Something that is **crooked** is bent or twisted.

bent
Shadha complained she couldn't get any juice through the **bent** straw, so the waiter got her another.

twisting
A **twisting** path led through the woods to the cottage.

warped
The wood was so **warped** they couldn't use it for anything but firewood.

cross ADJECTIVE

Someone who is **cross** is angry about something.

angry
Adrian was so **angry** he could hardly speak to her.

annoyed
Grandpa was **annoyed** when he found slugs had eaten his lettuces.

grumpy
Steven felt **grumpy** about not being well enough to go out.

irritable
Flies pestered the pony and made him very **irritable**.

cruel ADJECTIVE

Someone who is **cruel** hurts people or animals without caring.

brutal
The police said it was a **brutal** murder.

cold-hearted
The kidnapper was **cold-hearted** and ignored their pleas.

heartless
A **heartless** burglar smashed my grandma's favourite vase.

vicious
The burglar aimed a **vicious** kick at the guard dog.

ANTONYM: kind

crush VERB

To **crush** something is to destroy its shape by squeezing it.

flatten
They **flattened** the soft drink cans before recycling them.

screw up
Tibbles **screwed up** Mum's jacket when she slept on it.

squash
I dropped the shopping bag and **squashed** the tomatoes.

cry (1) VERB

To **cry** means to call out loudly.

call
*He **called**, "Anybody there?"*

shout
*"I can't hear you," she **shouted**.*

shriek
*"Oh no!" **shrieked** Libby. "My new jeans have shrunk."*

yell
*Debbie had to **yell** above the din in the school playground.*

cry (2) VERB

When you **cry**, tears come from your eyes and trickle down your face.

grizzle
*The baby **grizzles** when he's hungry.*

howl
*My sister **howled** when her gerbil died.*

snivel
*"It's no good **snivelling**," said the ugly sisters. "You're not going to the ball."*

sob
*Tommy **sobbed** when he dropped his ice cream.*

wail
*"I wanted to go to the pantomime!" **wailed** Roly.*

weep
*Lara **wept** as she waved goodbye.*

whimper
*The puppy **whimpered** when Abdul went off to school.*

cut (1) VERB

If you **cut** something, you use a knife or scissors to remove parts of it.

carve
*Nicholas **carved** the wood into the shape of a cat.*

chop
*The cook **chopped** an onion and carrot into small pieces.*

clip
*Katherine **clipped** out an advertisement from the newspaper.*

mow
*Grandpa loves **mowing** his lawn to keep it neat and tidy.*

prune
*Rose bushes need **pruning** in spring.*

saw
*The gardener **sawed** up some wood to make a nesting box.*

slice
*Mrs Cratchit always **sliced** the bread too thinly.*

snip
*The hairdresser **snipped** off my long hair.*

trim
*The barber carefully **trimmed** the wizard's long beard.*

cut (2) VERB

To **cut** can mean to reduce something.

lower
*The supermarket is **lowering** a lot of its prices this week.*

reduce
*The government is trying to **reduce** the amount of traffic on the roads.*

Dd

damage VERB
To **damage** something means to harm or spoil it.

break
*My little sister has **broken** her doll already.*

chip
*Melanie was furious when she **chipped** her nail varnish.*

dent
*A gatepost got in the way and **dented** Dad's bumper.*

destroy
*An unexpected storm **destroyed** their beach hut.*

ruin
*"You've **ruined** my painting!" David screamed angrily.*

scratch
*Natalie's bike was **scratched** when it fell in the holly bush.*

spoil
*The baby knocked over a cup and **spoiled** my homework.*

vandalize
*Someone has **vandalized** the phone box on the corner of our street.*

wreck
*Rocks often **wreck** boats that come too close to shore.*

dance VERB
When you **dance**, you move your body in time to music.

SOME KINDS OF DANCING:
ballet dancing
ballroom dancing:
  foxtrot
  quickstep
  tango
  waltz
break dancing
disco dancing
folk dancing
Highland dancing
Irish dancing
line dancing
salsa
square dancing
tap dancing

ballroom dancing

ballet dancing

break dancing

Irish dancing

disco dancing

tap dancing

dangerous ADJECTIVE

If something is **dangerous**, it is likely to harm you.

alarming
Rainforests are disappearing at an ***alarming*** *rate.*

deadly
The bite of some snakes can be ***deadly***.

harmful
Medicines can be ***harmful*** *if taken by the wrong person.*

menacing
The captain waved his hook at Peter in a ***menacing*** *fashion.*

risky
They decided the adventure was getting too ***risky***.

treacherous
Road conditions were ***treacherous*** *in the thick fog.*

unsafe
The bridge was rotten and ***unsafe*** *to cross.*

ANTONYM: safe

dark ADJECTIVE

When it is **dark**, there is not enough light to see properly.

black
The night was ***black*** *and stormy.*

dim
They could hardly see in the ***dim*** *hallway.*

gloomy
Rooms in the old castle were damp and ***gloomy***.

murky
The submarine moved slowly in the ***murky*** *depths of the ocean.*

shadowy
A ***shadowy*** *figure emerged from the misty woods.*

unlit
It looked as if no one was home as all the rooms were ***unlit***.

delicious ADJECTIVE

Food that is **delicious** tastes or smells very nice.

mouthwatering
At the village fair, the smell of frying onions was ***mouthwatering***.

scrumptious INFORMAL
When we got home from school, Mum made us a ***scrumptious*** *apple pie.*

tasty
Andrew enjoyed a ***tasty*** *snack on his way home from football training.*

ANTONYM: horrible

demonstrate (1) VERB

If someone **demonstrates** something, they show you how to do it.

explain
Jamie ***explained*** *how to separate the yolks and whites of eggs.*

illustrate
Our music teacher ***illustrated*** *how to play the violin.*

demonstrate (2) VERB

If people **demonstrate**, they hold a public meeting or march to show they are strongly for or against something.

march
Sometimes thousands of people ***march*** *in the capital to make their feelings known to the government.*

protest
When people ***protest***, *they often meet to carry banners and shout slogans.*

deserted

deserted ADJECTIVE
If a place is **deserted**, there are no people there.

abandoned
*In the middle of the wood, the boys came upon an **abandoned** cottage.*

empty
*They saw a farmhouse and ran towards it to ask for water, but it was **empty**.*

destroy VERB
To **destroy** something means to damage it so much it cannot be mended.

crush
*The cottages were **crushed** under the feet of the angry giant.*

damage
*A tree fell in the storm and **damaged** our garden shed.*

demolish
*Builders **demolished** an empty house to make space for a new theatre.*

ruin
*People complained that the new building **ruined** their view.*

smash
*The jetty was **smashed** when a motorboat went out of control.*

wreck
*Many ships used to be **wrecked** on rocks around the coast before lighthouses were built to signal warnings.*

different (1) ADJECTIVE
Something that is **different** from something else is not like it in one or more ways.

assorted
*I like boxes of **assorted** biscuits best.*

changed
*He seemed **changed** somehow. Perhaps it was the short hair.*

mixed
*Alex had **mixed** feelings about going up a grade at school.*

opposite
*Mum's quite **opposite** to me. She likes my room to be tidy and I like it to be a mess.*

various
*He had **various** excuses for being late.*

different (2) ADJECTIVE
Something **different** is unusual and out of the ordinary.

bizarre
*Have you seen Polly's new hairstyle? It's really **bizarre**!*

extraordinary
*The magician at the party performed some **extraordinary** tricks.*

peculiar
*There was something **peculiar** about the expression on his face.*

special
*I wanted to do something **special** for my seventh birthday.*

unusual
*The baby had an **unusual** cry.*

→ something else

dig VERB

When people or animals **dig**, they break up a surface.

burrow
Rabbits keep **burrowing** holes in the vegetable patch.

excavate
Archeologists are **excavating** at an ancient burial site.

hollow
Hollow out the centre of the pumpkin and cut teeth and eyeholes in the skin.

quarry
Marble has been **quarried** in Italy for many centuries.

scoop
Libby **scooped** out some ice cream from the tub.

tunnel
Some prisoners of war **tunnelled** their way out of the camp.

dirty ADJECTIVE

Something that is **dirty** is marked or covered with mud or stains.

filthy
"Your hands are **filthy**," said Dad. "Go and wash them."

foul
The pigsty was **foul** with droppings, old straw and mud.

greasy
"I hate washing up **greasy** dishes," complained Simon.

grimy
Driving in the open-top car was great fun, but it made their faces pretty **grimy**.

grubby
He scrubbed at his knees with a **grubby** old tissue.

messy
Cleaning out the hamster is a **messy** job.

muddy
He came in from football with **muddy** shorts and boots.

polluted
The city air is **polluted** with vehicle fumes.

stained
Their clothes and mouths were **stained** with blackberry juice.

untidy
Litter blew around the park and made it look **untidy**.

discover VERB

When you **discover** something, you find it or find out about it.

find
My brother has **found** a good way to train the new puppy.

uncover
Mehmet lifted some papers and **uncovered** a book he'd thought was lost.

unearth
Kylie was digging a hole in the garden and **unearthed** an old pot.

ANTONYM: hide

disguise

disguise VERB

If you **disguise** something, you change it so that people do not recognize it.

camouflage
The army **camouflages** tanks to hide them from aircraft.

conceal
She tried to **conceal** the spot on her chin.

cover
He **covered** his hair with a black wig.

dress up
"Is that your dad **dressed up** as Father Christmas?" asked Lucy.

mask
Dark sunglasses **masked** the expression in his eyes.

disturb (1) VERB

If you **disturb** someone, you interrupt them or spoil their peace and quiet.

bother
Don't **bother** me now, I'm busy.

hassle INFORMAL
"Quit **hassling** me, will you?" yelled my older sister.

interrupt
We're not allowed to **interrupt** Dad when he's working.

pester
Thomas **pestered** his brother in the library.

trouble
I don't want to **trouble** her now. She's watching her favourite programme.

disturb (2) VERB

If something **disturbs** you, it upsets or worries you.

alarm
I don't want to **alarm** you, but I think we should leave.

distress
The violence in the film **distressed** him.

frighten
The mouse was **frightened** when the cat sat by the cage.

upset
The noise **upset** the baby.

worry
Don't tell Grandma about the problem. It'll only **worry** her.

do (1) VERB

If you **do** something, you get on and finish it.

arrange
Dad is going to **arrange** everything.

carry out
The mechanic said he would **carry out** the repairs while we waited.

complete
"We should **complete** the work before the end of the week," said the builder.

cope with
Rachel's not sure she can **cope with** the decorations on her own.

finish
"You'll have to **finish** your homework before you go swimming," said Mum.

learn
What are you **learning** at the moment?

perform
Watch the clown **perform** his amazing juggling act.

do (2) VERB

If you say that something will **do**, you mean it is good enough.

be enough
*I wonder if half a page about my holidays will **be enough**?*

be sufficient
*I really hope this food will **be sufficient** for six people.*

be suitable
*Mum wanted to know if jeans would **be suitable** for the parents' evening.*

work
*They thought string might **work** as they didn't have any tape.*

drag VERB

If you **drag** a heavy object, you pull it along the ground.

draw
*The horse plodded on, **drawing** the heavy cart behind it.*

haul
*Fishermen **hauled** in their nets and found they had a large catch.*

pull
*Indigo **pulled** her friend from the river and rang for an ambulance.*

tow
*The farmer used a tractor to **tow** anything heavy around the farm.*

tug
*The boys **tugged** the sack of grain across the barn floor.*

draw (1) VERB

When you **draw**, you use something like a pencil or crayon to make a picture or a pattern.

doodle
*Holly **doodled** in her notebook as she listened to the teacher.*

paint
*I wanted to **paint** some pictures while I was on holiday.*

sketch
*In the field, an artist sat on a low stool **sketching** the scene.*

trace
*For homework we had to **trace** the outline of a map and fill in the rivers.*

draw (2) NOUN

A **draw** is the result in a game or competition in which nobody wins.

dead heat
*The result of the 100 metres sprint was a **dead heat**.*

tie
*Floella had hoped to win the competition, but there was a **tie** for first place.*

draw (3) VERB

If something **draws** you, it is so interesting that you move towards it.

attract
*A skydiving display **attracted** large crowds to the event.*

bring in
*We are hoping the advertising will **bring in** plenty of people.*

entice
*We were **enticed** into the shop by the display of cakes in the window.*

lure
*The witch **lured** the children into her house with promises of sweets.*

pull in
*The new programme has **pulled in** a lot of young viewers.*

dreadful

a
b
c
Dd
e
f
g
h
i
j
k
l
m
n
o
p
q
r
s
t
u
v
w
x
y
z

dreadful ADJECTIVE
Something that is **dreadful** is very bad or unpleasant.

alarming
*Our test results were pretty **alarming**.*

awful
*I was off school with an **awful** cold.*

dire
*The teacher issued **dire** warnings about the standard of our homework.*

frightening
*The force of the storm was **frightening**.*

frightful
*After the halloween party the house was in a **frightful** mess.*

ghastly
*A **ghastly** wail echoed round the castle.*

horrible
*The jumper I got for my birthday was a **horrible** yellow colour.*

dream NOUN
A **dream** is something you want very much.

ambition
*It's Michael's **ambition** to be a pilot.*

daydream
*My favourite **daydream** is being interviewed on TV about my book.*

fantasy
*Chelsea has this **fantasy** about being a famous model.*

→ vision

drink VERB
When you **drink**, you take liquid into your mouth and swallow it.

gulp
*Boris was so thirsty he **gulped** down all his lemonade.*

guzzle
*"Don't **guzzle** like that. Drink it slowly," said Granny.*

lap
*Tigger **lapped** up the milk Simon put down for him.*

sip
*Julia **sipped** the hot tea carefully.*

slurp
*Augustus greedily **slurped** the chocolate milk shake.*

swallow
*She **swallowed** the medicine without tasting it.*

swig
*They **swigged** cola from the bottle.*

DIFFERENT THINGS TO DRINK:

cold drinks	hot drinks
cola	cocoa
fizz	coffee
fruit juice	hot chocolate
lemonade	hot milk
milk	malted milk
milk shake	tea
smoothie	
soya milk	
squash	
water	

tea

lemonade

cola

milk

fruit juice

drive VERB

To **drive** means to make something or somebody go.

control
*Sharon **controlled** her car skilfully on the sandy beach.*

force
*The cruel baron **forced** the villagers from their cottages.*

push
*People at the front of the crowd were **pushed** forward.*

send
*Tom **sent** the ball over the fence.*

steer
*Rashid **steered** the go-kart into the side of the track.*

urge
*The knight **urged** his horse to a full gallop.*

dry ADJECTIVE

Something that is **dry** has no water in it at all.

arid
*Large areas of Mexico are **arid** desert.*

barren
*No crops could grow on the **barren** land.*

parched
*The garden was **parched** and all the seedlings died.*

dull (1) ADJECTIVE

Something that is **dull** is not interesting.

boring
*It was the most **boring** action film they'd ever seen.*

dreary
*I spent a **dreary** morning being dragged round the shops.*

tedious
*John found his cousin's story **tedious**.*

dull (2) ADJECTIVE

Something that is **dull** is not bright or clear.

cloudy
*The day was so **cloudy** we thought it might rain at any moment.*

dismal
*A most surprising thing happened on that **dismal** wintry afternoon.*

drab
*She wore a **drab** grey dress and grimy brown shoes.*

gloomy
*It was difficult to see the ogre in the **gloomy** light of the cave.*

grey
*The ugly duckling was a **grey** colour before he turned into a beautiful swan.*

miserable
*I like playing board games on **miserable**, rainy days.*

ANTONYM: bright

a
b
c
d
Ee
f
g
h
i
j
k
l
m
n
o
p
q
r
s
t
u
v
w
x
y
z

Ee

eager ADJECTIVE

If you are **eager**, you very much want to do or have something.

enthusiastic

*There were plenty of **enthusiastic** volunteers to help plan the school garden.*

impatient

*Mark was **impatient** to get back to school after the holidays.*

keen

*Brownie was **keen** to enter the competition at the dog show.*

longing

*Rachel was **longing** to see her newborn baby brother.*

easy ADJECTIVE

Something that is **easy** can be done without difficulty.

clear

*The way the teacher showed us made everything **clear**.*

obvious

*The answer to the problem was **obvious**. I gave Tom some of my ice cream and he stopped crying.*

plain

*It was **plain** to see he didn't like spiders.*

simple

*"Shelling the peas shouldn't take you long," said Mum. "It's a **simple** job."*

ANTONYM: **difficult**

eat VERB

When you **eat**, you chew and swallow food.

bite

*"**Bite** the jammy bit of the doughnut first," said Isaac.*

chew

*Cows **chew** the grass thoughtfully.*

devour

*They **devour** the sandwiches as fast as she makes them.*

gnaw

*Boggart happily lay down in the garden and **gnawed** his bone.*

gobble

*Mum told them to stop **gobbling** sweets.*

graze

*Sheep **graze** in the meadow until the farmer brings them in for the night.*

have a meal

*"We **have a meal** together every evening," said Mum.*

munch

*The horse likes to **munch** apples, carrots and oats.*

nibble

*Kylie **nibbles** her food like a mouse.*

peck

*Pigeons **peck** seeds and breadcrumbs thrown by the tourists.*

swallow

*Arthur was too busy talking to **swallow** his food properly.*

edge NOUN

An **edge** is the end or side of something.

border
*Her wallpaper had a **border** with animals on it.*

boundary
*The farmer planted a hedge along the **boundary** of his land.*

brim
*He filled his glass up to the **brim**.*

margin
*There were holes in the **margin** of the paper to fit the folder.*

rim
*They stood at the **rim** of the crater and gazed down into the depths.*

effort NOUN

Effort is the energy needed to do something.

energy
*It took a huge amount of **energy** to climb to the top of the hill.*

force
*With great **force**, the giant pushed a boulder from the mouth of the cave.*

struggle
*The boys found it a **struggle** to drag the heavy sack.*

work
*"They have put a lot of **work** into this project," said the teacher.*

empty (1) ADJECTIVE

Something that is **empty** has no people or things in it.

bare
*John's room was **bare** apart from a few packing cases.*

blank
*Hasan stared at the **blank** pages of his old diary.*

clear
*The road was **clear** and we arrived in record time.*

deserted
*We knocked on the door, but the place was completely **deserted**.*

unoccupied
*The house had been **unoccupied** for years.*

vacant
*We had a job to find a **vacant** field for our picnic.*

ANTONYM: full

empty (2) VERB

If you **empty** a container, you pour or take everything out of it.

clear out
*Dad started to **clear out** the shed today.*

drain
*There was a hole in his bucket and the water **drained** out.*

unload
*The children helped **unload** the car when they got home.*

ANTONYM: fill

encourage

encourage (1) VERB

If you **encourage** someone, you tell them that what they are doing is good.

cheer
However tired they get, the news they are winning always **cheers** them.

console
Jake finds drawing hard, but his teacher **consoles** him and he goes on trying.

reassure
Our dog is nervous of the water, and we have to **reassure** him.

encourage (2) VERB

To **encourage** something means to support it.

aid
Rain and sunshine **aid** the growth of plants in the garden.

help
My mum comes into school to **help** the little ones to read.

support
The head teacher **supports** our efforts to raise money for Children In Need.

end (1) NOUN

The **end** of a period of time or an event is the last part.

conclusion
The governors' meeting was brought to a swift **conclusion**.

ending
The **ending** of the story made me cry.

finish
Patrick was watching the match but he missed the **finish**.

ANTONYM: beginning

end (2) NOUN

The **end** of something is the furthest point of it.

back
Most damage was to the **back** of the bus.

point
The **point** of his pencil was always sharp.

rear
People in the **rear** carriage of the train were squashed together.

tip
Our cat shows her anger by twitching the **tip** of her tail.

end (3) VERB

If something **ends**, it finishes.

break up
School **breaks up** next week.

conclude
The minister **concluded** his speech by thanking his team.

finish
Luckily the play **finished** in time for us to catch the bus.

stop
Work **stopped** suddenly when the fire alarm sounded.

entertain VERB

If you **entertain** somebody, you do something they enjoy and find amusing.

amuse
Our baby is very easy to **amuse**, unless he's hungry or tired.

delight
The conjuror **delighted** everybody with his magical tricks.

occupy
Can you think of something to **occupy** the children while they are waiting?

please
She made a list of party games that would **please** her friends.

escape VERB

If a person or animal **escapes**, they get away from whatever is holding them.

bolt
The horse **bolted** before they could shut the stable door.

break free
The cage was locked but the hamster still managed to **break free**.

get away
She kept me talking and it was ages before I could **get away**.

run away
The police officer tried to make an arrest but the thief **ran away**.

run off
We tried to hang on to the stray dog but it **ran off**.

even (1) ADJECTIVE

If something is **even**, it is flat and level.

flat
The path was nice and **flat**.

level
They set up their football pitch on a **level** bit of ground.

smooth
The ice was **smooth** enough to skate on.

even (2) ADJECTIVE

If a contest is **even**, the two sides have the same chance of winning.

equal
The twins had an **equal** chance of winning the race.

level
The scores were **level** at half time.

➔ neck and neck

excitement NOUN

Excitement is feeling happy and unable to rest.

action
I love the **action** of an adventure holiday.

activity
There was plenty of **activity** going on in the games room.

commotion
We went to see what the **commotion** was all about.

thrills
They went on all the fairground rides in search of **thrills**.

extraordinary ADJECTIVE

Someone or something that is **extraordinary** is very special or unusual.

amazing
Ranjit came to the party wearing the most **amazing** gear.

bizarre
Her behaviour was totally **bizarre**.

odd
"That's an **odd** sight," said Mum. "Daffodils in August!"

strange
The magician's cloak was covered in **strange** designs.

unusual
It's **unusual** to see a kangaroo in a supermarket.

➔ out of this world

ANTONYM: ordinary

Ff

fade VERB

If something such as light, colour or sound **fades**, it becomes less strong.

bleach
*"Be careful drying your jeans outside," said Granny. "The sun might **bleach** them."*

die away
*The sound of clapping **died away**.*

grow dim
*Light in the room **grew dim**.*

vanish
*The buzzing noise **vanished** as soon as we stepped outside.*

fail (1) VERB

If someone **fails** when they try to do something, they cannot do it.

be defeated
*Nina hoped to win enough votes to be captain, but she **was defeated**.*

be in vain
*Robin's efforts to score a winning goal **were in vain**.*

be unsuccessful
*The head teacher's advertisement for more staff **was unsuccessful**.*

ANTONYM: **succeed**

fail (2) VERB

If something **fails**, it stops working or does not work so well.

give out
*Just when they needed it most, the washing machine **gave out**.*

sink
*When Gunnar realized he wasn't dreaming, his courage began to **sink**.*

stop working
*The computer **stopped working** and they couldn't print out their stories.*

faint ADJECTIVE

Something like a sound or mark that is **faint** is not easy to hear or see.

dim
*Light from the torch grew **dim** as the batteries failed.*

faded
*After several washes, lettering on the T-shirt became **faded**.*

indistinct
*They heard the sound of a voice but it was too **indistinct** to make out words.*

low
*Dark clouds filled the sky and there was a **low** rumble of thunder.*

vague
*He had a pleasant dream but it left only a **vague** memory.*

ANTONYM: **strong**

a b c d e Ff g h i j k l m n o p q r s t u v w x y z

fair (1) ADJECTIVE

Something that is **fair** seems reasonable to most people.

reasonable
*"We get a **reasonable** amount of pocket money," said Anthony.*

right
*He's got a bigger piece than me. It's just not **right**!*

ANTONYM: unfair

fair (2) ADJECTIVE

If someone's work is **fair**, it is about average.

average
*His work is **average**, neither good nor bad.*

not bad
*This is **not bad**, but you can do better when you try.*

satisfactory
*His performance in the football match was **satisfactory**.*

fair (3) ADJECTIVE

People who are **fair** have light-coloured hair or skin.

blond(e)
*My friend, Fiona, has straight **blonde** hair. I wish I had straight hair, mine's very curly.*

light
*Dorothea's hair is long and brown with **light** streaks.*

pale
*His **pale** skin burns easily in the sun so he keeps it covered up.*

fair (4) NOUN

A **fair** is an outdoor entertainment.

bazaar
*Maria bought her shawl at a **bazaar**.*

festival
*Here's our float for the May Day **festival**.*

fete
*The school **fete** was a great success.*

market
*Mum buys fruit at the local **market**.*

show
*The tractor company did well at the country **show**.*

faithful ADJECTIVE

If you are **faithful** to someone, you can be trusted and relied on.

devoted
*His dog was so **devoted** to him that she refused to leave when he was ill.*

loyal
*My sister only tells her secrets to people she knows are **loyal**.*

reliable
*You can count on **reliable** friends never to let you down.*

true
*Max is a footballer who will always be **true** to his team.*

trustworthy
*She may have a lovely smile, but is she a **trustworthy** member of the club?*

a
b
c
d
e
Ff
g
h
i
j
k
l
m
n
o
p
q
r
s
t
u
v
w
x
y
z

fall

fall (1) VERB

When someone or something **falls**, they drop towards the ground.

collapse
*Everybody screamed and laughed when the tent **collapsed**.*

crash
*The sign came loose and then **crashed** to the ground.*

crumple
*She burst into tears and **crumpled** in a heap.*

descend
*The pilot escaped from his burning plane and **descended** safely to the ground.*

dip
*The road **dipped** suddenly and they hit a sheet of water.*

drop
*She screamed and the tray **dropped** with a clatter.*

slip
*The precious vase **slipped** from his hands.*

stumble
*Hansel and Gretel **stumbled** several times on the rough path.*

trip
*Josephine **tripped** over the kerb and banged her knee.*

tumble
*The baby **tumbled** over as he tried to walk.*

→ come a cropper; drop like a stone

fall (2) VERB

To **fall** can mean to decrease in amount or value.

decrease
*Numbers of children at the school have **decreased** this year.*

drop
*The temperature **dropped** to freezing.*

go down
*Dad says my pocket money will **go down** if I'm not careful.*

→ plummet

ANTONYM: **rise**

false (1) ADJECTIVE

If something is **false**, it is not the real thing.

artificial
*The actress wore an **artificial** smile.*

bogus
*He spoke with a **bogus** American accent.*

fake
*The bank robber tried to leave the country using a **fake** passport.*

forged
*The letter had a **forged** signature.*

ANTONYM: **real**

false (2) ADJECTIVE

If something you say is **false**, it is not true.

incorrect
*Some of the details given by the suspect were **incorrect**.*

untrue
*I think the reason you've given for not doing your homework is **untrue**.*

wrong
*Rumours about the supermarket closing down are **wrong**.*

ANTONYM: **true**

fast (1) ADJECTIVE

Someone or something that is **fast** can move very quickly.

brisk
*Before lunch, Mum took us for a **brisk** walk in the park.*

express
*We got an **express** train to the city.*

high-speed
*I have a new **high-speed** computer.*

hurried
*After a **hurried** lunch we all went off to the cinema.*

quick
*The robbers managed a **quick** getaway.*

rapid
*The mouse made small, **rapid** movements.*

speedy
*When we saw Mum's face we made a **speedy** exit.*

swift
*With a **swift** action Jasmine leaped out of the car.*

→ jet-propelled

ANTONYM: **slow**

fast (2) ADVERB

If you do something **fast**, you do it quickly and without delay.

quickly
*The Gingerbread Man ran away **quickly** from the baker.*

rapidly
*The family walked **rapidly** through the churchyard.*

swiftly
*Goddard moved **swiftly** and silently after his enemy.*

→ in a flash; like a shot

ANTONYM: **slowly**

fast (3) ADVERB

If something is held **fast**, it is held firmly and strongly.

firmly
*The dog dragged Ben along, but he held **firmly** onto the lead.*

securely
*They tethered the goat **securely** to a post in the field.*

tightly
*Francesca held on **tightly** to the rabbit as its owner approached.*

fear

fear NOUN

Fear is the nasty feeling you have when you think you are in danger.

alarm
*Dom froze in **alarm** as a huge dog approached her.*

dread
*They waited in **dread** for the arrival of Aunt Agatha.*

fright
*He yelped in **fright** as the door burst open.*

horror
Horror gripped Matt as the dark form loomed above him.

panic
*Jack flew from the room in **panic**.*

terror
*Becky stared at the ghost in **terror**.*

feel (1) VERB

If you **feel** an object, you touch it to find out what it is like.

handle
*The princess looked thoughtful as she **handled** the velvet.*

stroke
*May I **stroke** the kitten's fur?*

touch
*I didn't want to **touch** the cactus. It looked prickly.*

feel (2) VERB

If you **feel** something, like happy or sad, that is how you are at that time.

be aware of
*Peter **was aware of** a nagging worry at the back of his mind.*

experience
*She **experienced** a sudden sense of loss.*

notice
*Max **noticed** a warm, happy feeling creeping over him.*

feel (3) VERB

If you **feel** something is the case, you believe it.

believe
*If I practise my writing, I **believe** I may become a novelist one day.*

consider
*Mum **considered** one cake was enough.*

judge
*I **judged** the baby would cry if we played with her for too long.*

think
*Everyone **thought** Meera would be good in the team.*

fierce ADJECTIVE

Something that is **fierce** is dangerous.

aggressive
*Even pets can become **aggressive** if they have new babies.*

dangerous
*Many large wild animals are **dangerous**, even when they look relaxed.*

ferocious
*The tiger's **ferocious** snarl frightened the other animals.*

savage
*You only have to watch wildlife programmes to see how **savage** lions can be.*

ANTONYM: gentle

fight find

fight (1) VERB
If you **fight** someone, you try to hurt them.

battle
*Tweedledum and Tweedledee **battled** over a rattle.*

brawl
*Some men were **brawling** in the street.*

grapple
*The old lady **grappled** with a boy who tried to steal her handbag.*

struggle
*John and David **struggled** for possession of the cricket bat.*

fight (2) NOUN
A **fight** is a fierce struggle.

battle
*There are lots of **battles** during a war.*

duel
*The two men settled their quarrel with a **duel**.*

fight (3) NOUN
A **fight** can be an angry disagreement.

argument
*A fierce **argument** broke out about who broke the vase.*

dispute
*There was a **dispute** over whose foot would fit the glass slipper.*

row
*Last week my parents had a **row**.*

squabble
*It was only a small **squabble**. They were soon friends again.*

find (1) VERB
When you **find** someone or something you have been looking for, you see them.

come across
*He thought he would **come across** the book if he kept looking.*

notice
*I knew he would **notice** the bright purple envelope.*

see
*A shop assistant was first to **see** the lost little boy.*

spot
*We hoped to **spot** our friend at the cinema.*

trace
*My dad has been trying to **trace** his long-lost brother.*

track down
*The police would soon **track down** their main suspect.*

find (2) VERB
To **find** can mean to learn or realize something.

become aware of
*If the police **become aware of** the motive, they can solve the crime.*

discover
*The princess won't be able to sleep until she **discovers** the pea under her mattress.*

learn
*"You **learn**," said Jason, "that it's a bad idea to get on the wrong side of him."*

realize
*"When did you **realize** you'd lost your wallet?" asked the restaurant manager.*

fine

fine (1) ADJECTIVE
Something that is **fine** is extremely good.

beautiful
There was a **beautiful** view of the forest from the hotel window.

excellent
Julia tried very hard and produced an **excellent** piece of work.

magnificent
The gardens at the country house were really **magnificent**.

outstanding
The class gave an **outstanding** performance at the concert.

splendid
After the match, Uncle Albert gave us a **splendid** meal.

fine (2) ADJECTIVE
Fine can mean small in size or thickness.

delicate
The bride's veil was made of such a **delicate** material it hardly seemed to be there.

lightweight
Lightweight seeds from the dandelion heads blew across the garden.

powdery
Dust lay in a **powdery** film on every surface in the room.

thin
Spiders can produce perfect webs with **thin** threads.

finish VERB
When you **finish** something, you reach the end of it.

close
The piece of music **closed** with a roll of drums and a clash of cymbals.

complete
Sanjay **completed** his poem and read it out to his friends.

conclude
"I will **conclude** this talk," said the Mayor, "by thanking my staff."

end
Hannah's party **ended** with a colourful firework display.

stop
The test came to an end and the children **stopped** writing.

ANTONYM: start

firm (1) ADJECTIVE
Something that is **firm** does not move easily when you press or push it.

hard
This pear's not ripe. It's still **hard**.

rigid
The bodybuilder's muscles were **rigid**.

set
Now the glue is **set**, it should be okay.

firm (2) ADJECTIVE
Something that is **firm** does not shake or move.

secure
The engineer made sure the nuts and bolts were **secure**.

solid
The table was **solid** enough to climb on.

firm (3) ADJECTIVE

If someone is **firm**, they will not change their mind.

definite
*I can take that as a **definite** "no" then?*

strict
*One of our teachers at school is very **strict** about noise.*

unshakable
*The doctor has an **unshakable** belief in lots of exercise.*

fit (1) VERB

If something **fits** something else, it is right for it.

belong to
*This cap **belongs to** the green bottle.*

be suitable
*We wanted some shoes that **were suitable** for school.*

go with
*According to the instructions, this bit **goes with** that.*

match
*Joe needed a bit of jigsaw to **match** the edge pieces.*

fit (2) ADJECTIVE

Someone who is **fit** is healthy.

healthy
*Grandma's **healthier** than some people half her age.*

strong
*Calum's **strong** as an ox.*

well
*He's **well** enough to carry on training.*

fix (1) VERB

If you **fix** something somewhere, you put it there firmly.

attach
*A caterpillar **attaches** itself to a plant to spin its cocoon.*

fasten
*The suspect's wrists were **fastened** together with handcuffs.*

secure
*He **secured** his bike to the stand with a padlock and chain.*

stick
*Pat **stuck** a stamp on the envelope.*

fix (2) VERB

If you **fix** something that has broken, you make it work again.

mend
*I had to **mend** my model aircraft after it crashed.*

patch up
*We managed to **patch up** the airbed.*

repair
*Holly found someone who could **repair** her computer.*

flow VERB

If liquid **flows** in a certain direction, it moves there steadily.

cascade
*I forgot to turn off the tap and water **cascaded** all over the floor.*

flood
*The river broke its banks and **flooded** across the fields.*

leak
*We need a new tank. Water's **leaking** from the old one.*

pour
*Rain **poured** from the choked gutters and soaked the walls.*

spurt
*Blood **spurted** from his wound.*

flower

flower NOUN

A **flower** is the part of the plant that has coloured petals. When the petals fade, fruit or seeds develop.

WILD FLOWERS:

bluebell   dandelion
buttercup   foxglove
daisy   primrose

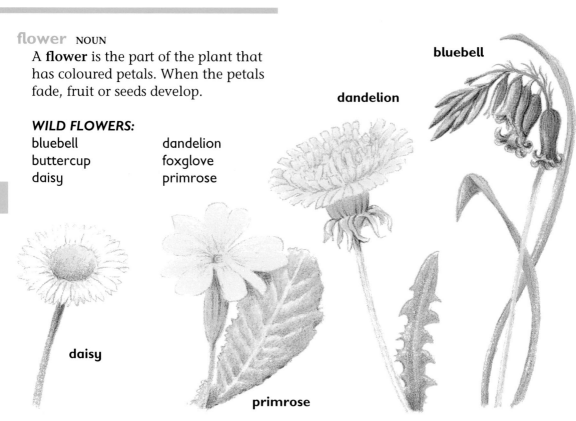

bluebell

dandelion

daisy

primrose

GARDEN FLOWERS:

chrysanthemum   rose
crocus   snowdrop
daffodil   sunflower
geranium   tulip
hollyhock   violet
lily   wallflower
pansy

sunflower

lily

daffodil

rose

fluffy ADJECTIVE

Something that is **fluffy** is very soft and light.

feathery
*Snow fell in **feathery** flakes, white against the dark sky.*

furry
*Jamilla gently stroked the kitten's **furry** black coat.*

light
*Her angora jumper was wonderfully **light** and warm.*

soft
*The **soft** white bread was still warm from the oven.*

fly VERB

When a bird, insect or aircraft **flies**, it moves through the air.

flutter
*A butterfly **fluttered** towards a flower.*

glide
*An owl **glides** silently above the corn.*

soar
*The plane **soars** to about a thousand metres before it levels out.*

swoop
*We watched a hawk **swoop** down and rise again with something in its claws.*

fold VERB

If you **fold** something, you bend it so that one part lies over another.

bend
*He wrote on the envelope, "Photographs. Please do not **bend**."*

crease
*The instructions told him to **crease** along the dotted line.*

crumple
*Ben **crumpled** the note and put it away in his pocket.*

tuck
*Mum showed me how to **tuck** in the sheet.*

follow (1) VERB

If you **follow** someone who is moving, you move along behind them.

chase
*William **chased** me as far as the gate, then gave up.*

pursue
*The police **pursued** the suspect and soon caught him.*

shadow
*A detective **shadowed** her throughout the afternoon.*

tail
*We **tailed** him for hours, but lost him in the crowd.*

track
*The gamekeeper showed us the best way to **track** deer.*

follow (2) VERB

If one thing **follows** another, it happens after it.

come after
*Games usually **come after** lunch.*

come next
*We enjoyed the clowns and wondered what would **come next**.*

follow (3) VERB

If you **follow** something such as an explanation, you understand it.

grasp
*Hugh **grasped** the idea quite quickly when the teacher explained it.*

realize
*She finally **realized** what her dad was getting at.*

take in
*For a moment he could not **take in** what she was saying.*

understand
*The explanation was clear enough. I **understood** it at once.*

→ get the picture

a
b
c
d
e
Ff
g
h
i
j
k
l
m
n
o
p
q
r
s
t
u
v
w
x
y
z

foolish

foolish ADJECTIVE

Something or somebody **foolish** is silly or unwise.

daft INFORMAL

*Emily said it would be **daft** to go out in that weather without a coat.*

idiotic

*He's always got some **idiotic** plan that is sure to go wrong.*

mad

*It was a **mad** idea, but we agreed it might just work.*

silly

*I don't like the **silly** things she does, so I'm not her friend any more.*

unwise

*Our cat is anxious about her new kittens and it's **unwise** to touch them.*

force NOUN

The **force** of something is the powerful effect it has.

impact

*With the **impact** of the storm, trees crashed and roofs were blown off.*

might

*They fought the battle with the **might** of two thousand soldiers.*

power

*The giant used all his **power** to uproot the tree.*

strength

*Slowly, the **strength** of the wind faded and they were able to leave their shelter.*

violence

*He was powerful, but he was against using **violence** to achieve his ends.*

fragile ADJECTIVE

Something that is **fragile** is easily broken or damaged.

breakable

*They wrapped all the **breakable** things in sheets of newspaper.*

brittle

*Fine china teacups are **brittle** and are not usually for every day.*

delicate

*My sister's wedding cake was covered in **delicate** sugar rosebuds.*

flimsy

*The framework of the tent was too **flimsy** and it collapsed.*

frail

*As he clambered into the **frail** boat, it rocked and almost threw him out.*

thin

*Oliver's legs looked **thin**, as if they would hardly bear his weight.*

fresh ADJECTIVE

If something feels **fresh**, it is clean, cool and refreshing.

bracing

*After lunch we needed a walk in the **bracing** sea air.*

clean

*Back home after camping, the best thing was to sleep in **clean** sheets.*

clear

*They breathed in the **clear** early morning air outside the cottage.*

pure

*We drank deeply of the **pure** water that bubbled up from the spring.*

friend NOUN

A **friend** is someone you know well and like very much.

ally
*In a fight, it is as well to know who are your **allies**.*

companion
*The old lady's only **companion** was a large dog.*

mate INFORMAL
*Samuel can usually be found talking to his **mates**.*

playmate
*Meera's **playmates** waited for her to finish lunch.*

friendly ADJECTIVE

If you are **friendly** to someone, you behave in a kind and pleasant way to them.

affectionate
*The letter from Simon was **affectionate**, with kisses at the end.*

amiable
*There are lots of **amiable** people working at our supermarket.*

close
*Amy and her sister Rosie are very **close** and go everywhere together.*

kind
*I enjoy going to the dentist because she's so **kind**.*

loving
*Emma always gives her grandma a **loving** hug when they meet.*

welcoming
*Mrs Jones opened the front door and greeted them with a **welcoming** smile.*

frighten VERB

If something **frightens** you, it makes you afraid.

alarm
*Don't let that sound **alarm** you. It's only a ghost rattling its chains.*

scare
*The dog **scared** me when it snarled and moved forward.*

shock
*I was **shocked** when a bear stopped to talk to me.*

startle
*The sudden bang **startled** him.*

terrify
*Fireworks **terrify** our cat.*

→ make your blood run cold; make your flesh creep

frightened ADJECTIVE

Someone who is **frightened** thinks that something nasty might happen.

afraid
*Who's **afraid** of the big bad wolf?*

alarmed
*Ben was **alarmed** when he heard something tapping at the window.*

scared
*Miss Muffet was **scared** when a spider sat down beside her.*

startled
*The pony was **startled** when a paper bag blew across its path.*

terrified
*One of the new ducklings is **terrified** of water.*

fruit

fruit NOUN

A **fruit** is the part of a plant that develops from the flower and contains the seeds. Many fruits are good to eat.

KINDS OF FRUITS:

apple	lemon	peach
avocado	lime	pear
banana	mango	pineapple
blueberry	melon	plum
cherry	orange	raspberry
grape	papaya	strawberry
grapefruit	passion fruit	tomato
kiwi fruit		

apple

bananas

grapes

lemon

kiwi fruits

mango

orange

passion fruits

full (1) ADJECTIVE

Full can mean leaving nothing out.

complete
*Marty has got a **complete** set of Harry Potter books.*

entire
*My dad has sold his **entire** collection of stamps.*

whole
*The teacher said she wanted to hear the **whole** story.*

pineapple

strawberries

full (2) ADJECTIVE

If something is **full**, there is no room for anything more.

brimming
*The glass of milk was **brimming**, so he lifted it carefully.*

bulging
*Jo's shopping bag was **bulging**.*

crammed
*The bus was **crammed** and Josh couldn't get on.*

crowded
*The cafe was **crowded**, so we went to the park instead.*

heaped
*She came back with a **heaped** plate.*

packed
*When we arrived, the hall was **packed**.*

fun NOUN

Fun is something enjoyable that makes you feel happy.

amusement
*They got a lot of **amusement** from watching the puppies play.*

enjoyment
*In Ratty's opinion, lots of **enjoyment** could be had messing about in boats.*

entertainment
*The best part of the **entertainment** was watching the tightrope walker.*

pleasure
*His idea of **pleasure** was sitting quietly on the beach.*

funny (1) ADJECTIVE

Funny people or things make you laugh.

amusing
*Grandma finds cartoons **amusing**.*

comical
*I liked the clown. Even his face was **comical**.*

hilarious
*David told us this **hilarious** story.*

humorous
*Mai Lin likes **humorous** books best.*

ridiculous
*His uncle wore a **ridiculous** green hat to the party.*

witty
*Our teacher often says **witty** things.*

funny (2) ADJECTIVE

Something that is **funny** is rather strange or surprising.

odd
*I had an **odd** feeling something was going to happen.*

peculiar
*When she woke up, Heather had a **peculiar** expression on her face.*

strange
*The old man was wearing **strange** clothes.*

unusual
*The house had an **unusual** name.*

weird
*He was very tall and thin, and was dressed in a **weird** cloak.*

a
b
c
d
e
Ff
g
h
i
j
k
l
m
n
o
p
q
r
s
t
u
v
w
x
y
z

Gg

game NOUN

A **game** is something you play for sport or fun. Most games have rules.

amusement
What **amusements** have we got for the little ones?

competition
Claudette won first prize in the **competition**.

contest
There was an arm-wrestling **contest** and I won.

entertainment
The only available **entertainment** was snakes and ladders.

match
Our team is bound to win the football **match** this afternoon.

gap (1) NOUN

A **gap** is a space between two things, or a hole in something solid.

break
The sun shone brightly through a **break** in the clouds.

chink
Chinks were appearing in the old fence.

crack
Every room had **cracks** in the plaster.

hole
A rabbit had dug a **hole** under the fence.

space
They tried to find a **space** in the hedge to look through.

gap (2) NOUN

A **gap** is a period of time when you stop doing something.

interval
There was an **interval** of fifteen minutes after the first act.

lull
Jade waited for a **lull** in the conversation so that she could say something.

pause
There was a short **pause** before the head teacher spoke again.

gasp VERB

When you **gasp**, you take a short quick breath through your mouth.

breathe heavily
When they reached the top of the hill, they were **breathing heavily**.

choke
The firemen found a woman **choking** in the dense smoke.

pant
"Quick!" she **panted**. "I must have a drink of water."

puff
They **puffed** and groaned as they finished the race.

wheeze
Paul was **wheezing** and coughing because of his very bad cold.

gather (1) VERB

If people or animals **gather**, they come together in a group.

assemble
*Students were asked to **assemble** in the hall for a special announcement.*

crowd round
*A woman fell and passers-by **crowded round** to help or offer advice.*

flock
*He was such a good speaker, people would **flock** from miles around to hear him.*

meet
*Parties are wonderful places to **meet** and have fun.*

gather (2) VERB

If you **gather** things, you collect them from different places.

accumulate
*"I don't know how I've managed to **accumulate** all this rubbish," Mum said.*

bring together
*They were told to **bring together** all the things they could find beginning with the letter "B".*

collect
*In the autumn the children **collected** leaves of different colours.*

hoard
*My grandpa **hoards** things he's sure will come in useful one day.*

stockpile
*During a war, people often **stockpile** tins of food.*

gather (3) VERB

If you **gather** something, you learn or believe it.

believe
*I **believe** they're putting traffic lights on that dangerous corner at last.*

hear
*We **hear** there's going to be a new teacher next term.*

learn
*She **learned** that her cousin was getting married in the spring.*

understand
*I **understand** we're to have a new swimming pool.*

general ADJECTIVE

You use **general** to say that something is true in most cases.

accepted
*The **accepted** feeling is that pollution is a dangerous thing.*

broad
*You can often tell which TV programmes will have a **broad** appeal.*

common
*It is **common** knowledge that swimming is good for you.*

usual
*The **usual** behaviour of children at this school is very good.*

widespread
*There is a **widespread** understanding of the need to recycle.*

a
b
c
d
e
f
Gg
h
i
j
k
l
m
n
o
p
q
r
s
t
u
v
w
x
y
z

gentle

gentle ADJECTIVE
Someone who is **gentle** is kind, calm and sensitive.

calm
Mum has a **calm** voice, even when she's feeling angry.

kind
The nurse who looked after me was very **kind**.

soft-hearted
Simon's a **soft-hearted** little boy. He would hate to upset anyone.

tender
She gazed at the baby with a **tender** smile.

get (1) VERB
If you **get** something, you fetch it or are given it.

be given
I hope I **am given** a bike for my birthday.

bring
They weren't sure what food to **bring** for the picnic.

buy
We didn't know what to **buy** Annabel for her birthday.

collect
Susan went to **collect** interesting shells from the beach.

earn
How much money do paper boys **earn**?

fetch
The dragon likes **fetching** our paper, but he always sets light to it.

gather
They went to **gather** wood for the fire.

win
He's not very good at sums, but he **wins** a prize for his poetry every year.

get (2) VERB
Get often means the same as become or arrive.

arrive
My brother **arrives** home in time for dinner most nights.

become
Evenings **become** darker much earlier in winter.

come
We reached the platform before the train **came** in.

grow
The sky was **growing** lighter as the sun came up.

reach
"Can you **reach** that tin on the top shelf, please?" asked Gran.

turn
The leaves are **turning** redder every day.

ghost NOUN
A **ghost** is a shadowy figure of someone no longer living that some people believe they see.

phantom
Ron gasped. "It's the **phantom** that haunts the castle!"

spectre
Hamlet saw the **spectre** of his dead father.

spirit
"I don't believe in **spirits**," Danny said.

spook
The boys went out **spook** hunting.

gift NOUN

A **gift** is a present.

contribution
*Our teacher was collecting **contributions** for children in hospital.*

donation
*A **donation** from the parents helped the school buy more books.*

offering
*The primroses were only a small **offering** but Mum was really pleased.*

present
*Everyone brought a **present** when they came to the party.*

give VERB

If you **give** someone something, you hand it to them or provide it for them.

contribute
*Auntie Charlotte often **contributes** to animal charities.*

donate
*Several parents were able to **donate** prizes for the raffle.*

hand over
***Hand over** your mobile to the teacher before you go into class.*

offer
*She decided to **offer** me one of her sweets.*

present
*One of the school governors came to **present** a prize for swimming.*

provide
*The cat-rescue people asked us to **provide** tins of cat food.*

supply
*When it rains, my teacher always **supplies** drawing paper to the class.*

gloomy (1) ADJECTIVE

If a place is **gloomy**, it is dark and dull.

dark
*The room was **dark**, with cobwebs hanging down everywhere.*

dismal
*It was a **dismal** landscape with hardly any trees or bushes.*

dreary
*She lived in a **dreary** town full of dirty grey buildings.*

gloomy (2) ADJECTIVE

If people are **gloomy**, they are unhappy and not at all hopeful.

dejected
*She felt **dejected** when she didn't win.*

glum
*Angela felt **glum** when the time came to leave her new pet friend.*

sad
*After his gerbil died, John felt **sad**.*

→ down in the dumps

glow VERB

If something **glows**, it shines with a steady dull light.

gleam
*The polished brass knocker **gleamed** in the torchlight.*

glimmer
*It was getting dark when they saw a light **glimmering** in a cottage window.*

shine
*The paintwork on Dad's new car **shone** in the sunlight.*

smoulder
*The remains of the bonfire were still **smouldering** the next day.*

glue

glue NOUN

Glue is a thick sticky liquid used for joining things together.

adhesive
*By the time they finished, their fingers were sticky with **adhesive**.*

cement
*I need some **cement** for my model aircraft.*

gum
*Nicola spread **gum** carefully on the back of her drawing.*

paste
*"We'll use this **paste** to make our collages," said the art teacher.*

go (1) VERB

If you **go** somewhere, you move or travel there.

depart
*Fred saw his sister **depart** in a flurry of bags and cases.*

disappear
*I watched Dad **disappear** downstairs to get my supper.*

leave
*"He'll **leave** as soon as we mention the washing-up," said Auntie.*

travel
*I would like to **travel** round the world when I'm older.*

vanish
*We watched the magician **vanish** in a puff of smoke.*

go (2) VERB

If something such as a watch **goes**, it works properly.

function
*This won't **function** without batteries.*

work
*My watch doesn't **work** because I dropped it in the bath.*

go (3) VERB

If something **goes** with something else, they belong together.

belong
*Where does this screw **belong**?*

fit
*I think that bit of the jigsaw **fits** there.*

go (4) NOUN

A **go** is an attempt to do something.

attempt
*The dung beetle failed to take off on the first **attempt**.*

shot
*"I'd like another **shot** at that. I'm sure I can do it," said Mary.*

stab
*Sue had a **stab** at making a clay pot, but it collapsed in a heap.*

try
*Move the target closer before you have another **try**.*

turn
*"That's not fair!" cried Marta. "It's my **turn** next!"*

good

good (1) ADJECTIVE

If something like a book or film is **good**, people like it.

brilliant
*The new action film was **brilliant**.*

enjoyable
*We had an **enjoyable** afternoon playing on the swings.*

excellent
*It was an **excellent** game of football but it ended in a draw.*

exciting
*Robert had such an **exciting** ride on the big dipper.*

fabulous
*Our holiday trip to the theme park was really **fabulous**.*

fantastic
*The magician showed the audience some **fantastic** tricks.*

great
*It was such a **great** film, that Lewis wanted to see it again.*

gripping
*It was a **gripping** story. Floella couldn't put the book down.*

thrilling
*Most of the film was boring but it had a **thrilling** ending.*

wonderful
*Thomas sighed happily. "It's been a **wonderful** day. Thank you."*

good (2) ADJECTIVE

Someone who is **good** at something is skilful and successful at it.

bright
*Sam's really **bright** at history. He always comes top.*

clever
*Mum's **clever** with plants. Everything grows for her.*

expert
*You need an **expert** plumber to sort out that tangle of pipes.*

skilful
*The juggler was so **skilful** he could keep several plates in the air at once.*

skilled
*Our doctor is very **skilled**. He knew at once what to do.*

talented
*The music teacher thought Julian was a **talented** violinist.*

good (3) ADJECTIVE

A child or animal that is **good** is well-behaved and obedient.

polite
*Robin was always **polite** when his family had visitors.*

well-behaved
*My dog is **well-behaved**. He never tries to run away.*

good (4) ADJECTIVE

Someone who is **good** is kind and caring and can be trusted.

caring
*My grandma is a gentle, **caring** person.*

helpful
*That lady gave us some **helpful** advice.*

kind
*My knee hurt but the nurse was very **kind**.*

thoughtful
*"Thanks for the cup of tea," said Mum. "It was **thoughtful** of you."*

grab VERB

If you **grab** something, you take hold of it suddenly and roughly.

clutch
*She **clutched** at her bag before the thief could make off with it.*

grasp
*The old lady **grasped** the handrail to stop herself falling down the steps.*

seize
*Mark **seized** his jacket and flew out of the door.*

snatch
*Joel **snatched** a sandwich before his mum could stop him.*

graceful ADJECTIVE

Someone or something that is **graceful** moves in a smooth, pleasant way.

effortless
*She turned towards them with an **effortless** swing of her body.*

elegant
*The famous actress crossed the stage with **elegant** movements.*

flowing
*His pencil quickly covered the page with **flowing** lines.*

smooth
*They stood watching the **smooth** glide of a swan on the river.*

supple
*Dancers moved around each other with **supple** ease.*

grateful ADJECTIVE

If you are **grateful** for something that someone has done, you want to thank them.

appreciative
*Mum likes having my friends to tea because they're so **appreciative**.*

indebted
*They felt **indebted** to the old man for all the help he had given them.*

obliged
*"I'm **obliged** to you," said the fairy, as Mary freed her from the cobweb.*

thankful
*We were **thankful** to see supper was ready because we were ravenous.*

grave ADJECTIVE

Something that is **grave** is important, serious and worrying.

gloomy
*We knew the news was bad as soon as we saw his **gloomy** expression.*

serious
*"I'm afraid her condition is **serious**," said the doctor.*

solemn
*The head teacher made the announcement in **solemn** tones.*

sombre
*I noticed the postman looked unusually **sombre** today.*

worrying
*There was a **worrying** lack of medical supplies in the war zone.*

great (1) ADJECTIVE

You say something is **great** when it is large in size, number or amount.

colossal
*The Titanic was a **colossal** ship in height and width.*

enormous
*Charles took his **enormous** pet out for a walk.*

gigantic
*The whole thing was a **gigantic** muddle.*

huge
*I think I've made a **huge** mistake.*

immense
*To Jackson's **immense** relief, the puppy was saved.*

mammoth
*The toyshop has got a **mammoth** sale on.*

vast
*They came across a **vast** area where nothing grew.*

great (2) ADJECTIVE

Great also means important.

celebrated
*Picasso painted many **celebrated** pictures.*

famous
*We need someone **famous** to address the crowd.*

grand
*A **grand** staircase curved upwards from the hall.*

important
*Sir Isaac Newton was an **important** scientist and mathematician.*

great (3) ADJECTIVE

Great can mean wonderful.

excellent
*Sirah had an **excellent** time on her beach holiday in Greece.*

fantastic
*"The skateboarding display was **fantastic**," said Jacob.*

terrific
*We gave our teacher a **terrific** send-off when she left to have a baby.*

tremendous
*The film was **tremendous**. It really scared my dad.*

greedy ADJECTIVE

Someone who is **greedy** wants more than they need of something.

gluttonous
*They were horrified by the ogre's **gluttonous** behaviour at dinner.*

grasping
*Scrooge was a **grasping** old man who hoarded his money.*

piggish
*Nobody likes him because of the **piggish** way he gobbles his food.*

selfish
*She's a **selfish** little girl who won't share her toys.*

voracious
*I'm surprised Beth is such a small baby because she has a **voracious** appetite.*

grief

grief NOUN

Someone who feels **grief** is very sad, often because a person or animal they love has died.

distress
When Michel's best friend moved away they both showed signs of **distress**.

heartache
He wasn't prepared for the **heartache** that followed the death of his hamster.

misery
We couldn't find any way of helping Daniel get over his **misery**.

sadness
It was the **sadness** in her eyes that told us what had happened.

sorrow
It was a time of great **sorrow** for the whole family.

grim ADJECTIVE

If someone looks **grim**, they seem worried or angry about something.

bad-tempered
Mr Jones had a **bad-tempered** expression when he handed back our ball.

grave
The head teacher looked **grave** when he told us about the accident.

serious
Tim knew something was wrong when he saw her **serious** face.

severe
His mouth was set in a **severe** line. "What have you been up to?" he asked.

unfriendly
I try not to go in that shop because the man always looks so **unfriendly**.

ground NOUN

The **ground** is the surface of the earth or the floor of a room.

dirt
She dropped her bread jam-side-down on the **dirt**.

earth
It hadn't rained for more than three weeks and the **earth** was parched.

land
The **land** at the back of the house looked perfect for a small garden.

soil
The gardener spent the morning digging the **soil**.

group (1) NOUN

A **group** of things or people is a number of them that are linked together in some way.

crowd
We looked at the **crowd** of people gathered around him.

mob
A **mob** of monkeys attacked the car.

party
At lunchtime a **party** of elderly people arrived in a coach.

group (2) VERB

To **group** things or people means to link them together.

arrange
I **arranged** my books neatly in alphabetical order.

organize
We had to **organize** ourselves into teams.

OTHER GROUPS:
a bunch of grapes
a clutch of eggs
a flock of sheep
a herd of cows
a litter of puppies
a pack of wolves
a pride of lions
a school of dolphins
a shoal of fish
a swarm of bees

a flock of sheep

a pack of wolves

a pride of lions

a school of dolphins

a shoal of fish

grow

grow (1) VERB

To **grow** means to increase in size or amount.

develop
Acorns develop into oak trees.

expand
Our local bookshop is expanding now people are buying more books.

get bigger
When you get bigger, you'll understand.

get taller
Once I get taller I'll be able to reach that high shelf.

increase
The number of people coming to live in the village is increasing.

multiply
The number of rabbits tends to multiply rapidly in spring.

grow (2) VERB

When plants **grow**, they are alive and do well.

flourish
Cacti flourish when you don't water them too much.

germinate
Grass seeds germinate quite quickly.

spring up
Weeds seemed to spring up the minute she turned her back.

sprout
During the spring, leaves begin to sprout everywhere.

grow (3) VERB

To **grow** can mean to change gradually.

become
At night in the desert it becomes much colder.

get
The boys were getting hungry.

turn
The seedlings gradually turned into tall plants with beautiful flowers.

guard VERB

If you **guard** a person or object, you stay near them to keep them safe.

protect
*Nicholas was always ready to **protect** his younger brother.*

shelter
*Tender young plants need **sheltering** from the frost.*

shield
*They wore hats to **shield** them from the harmful rays of the sun.*

watch over
*The dog was left to **watch over** the house while they were out.*

guess VERB

If you **guess** something, you give an answer without knowing if it is right.

believe
*"I **believe** our house is about ten metres high," said Abdullah.*

estimate
*Can you **estimate** how long this cleaning job will take?*

imagine
*"I **imagine** he's missed the train again," said Petra.*

suppose
*Mum said, "I **suppose** you're too tired to watch TV, then?"*

suspect
*I **suspect** he didn't intend to come.*

think
*They **thought** the new music teacher would be older.*

guide (1) VERB

If you **guide** someone, you show them where to go or what to do.

accompany
*We'll need an adult to **accompany** us through the wood.*

direct
*It was a complicated journey and people had to **direct** them at every turn.*

escort
*The teacher promised to **escort** Ben.*

lead
*Lawrence offered to **lead** the others because he'd been there before.*

steer
*Karen discovered it's not all that easy to **steer** a pony.*

usher
*A lady with a torch **ushered** us to our cinema seats.*

guide (2) VERB

If someone or something **guides** you, they affect what you do.

advise
*My sister says the school will **advise** her on a choice of career.*

affect
*The weather will **affect** our plans for a picnic.*

influence
*Matt will be **influenced** by his brother.*

guilty ADJECTIVE

If you feel **guilty**, you are unhappy because you have done something wrong.

ashamed
*Rachel felt **ashamed** about her behaviour.*

sheepish
*The boys looked **sheepish** when their mum saw the mess.*

sorry
*I felt **sorry** about making the baby cry.*

a
b
c
d
e
Gg
h
i
j
k
l
m
n
o
p
q
r
s
t
u
v
w
x
y
z

Hh

habit NOUN

A **habit** is something you do often, sometimes without thinking about it.

custom
It was his custom to take the dog for a walk every night after supper.

routine
She cleaned the house every day as a matter of routine.

tradition
It has become a tradition to go to Grandma's for Sunday lunch.

way
It is Dad's way to polish the car at the weekend.

hairy ADJECTIVE

Something or someone **hairy** is covered in hair.

bristly
Dad rubbed his bristly chin thoughtfully. "I think I can manage that," he said.

furry
A hamster is a small furry rodent that sleeps during the day.

shaggy
Our dog has got a long shaggy coat.

woolly
I had a nice woolly jacket for my birthday.

handle (1) VERB

If you **handle** something, you touch or feel it with your hands.

feel
She liked to feel the cool sand as she built sandcastles on the beach.

finger
Don't finger that pear unless you're going to eat it.

hold
He liked picking up spiders, but they were difficult to hold.

stroke
Lily stroked the kitten and made it purr.

touch
We touched the baby hamsters gently.

handle (2) VERB

If you agree to **handle** something, you say you will do it.

control
The teacher asked him to control the sale of tickets at the door.

cope with
Can you cope with the plates while I make the tea?

deal with
Sebastian offered to deal with the washing-up.

look after
Mrs Smith said she would look after the flower arrangements.

manage
Will you be able to manage the rest if I leave now?

supervise
I need to supervise the face painting.

hang VERB

If you **hang** something up, you fix it so that it does not touch the ground.

drape
Trudy draped a blanket around her shoulders to keep out the cold.

fasten
Spencer fastened a large picture above the fireplace.

fix
We couldn't decide where to fix the mirror in the bathroom.

suspend
They suspended a lantern from inside the top of the tent.

happen VERB

If something **happens**, it takes place.

arise
If anything should arise that causes problems, let the teacher know.

come about
I don't know how it came about, but I found I was in charge.

crop up
You never know what can crop up at a time like this.

occur
It was beginning to get dark when the incident occurred.

take place
Where exactly are you expecting this party to take place?

happy ADJECTIVE

If you are **happy**, you feel good because most things are the way you want.

bright
She always has a bright smile for everyone she meets.

cheerful
It rained all day, but Dad was still bright and cheerful.

contented
The others moaned, but Jeremiah was quite contented.

delighted
Mum was delighted with her present.

glad
I'm glad our new teacher is friendly.

joyful
The dog gave a joyful bark as soon as he saw Tim.

light-hearted
The musical we performed was a light-hearted affair.

overjoyed
Dan was overjoyed at the results of his hard work.

pleased
Esther was really pleased to be going home again.

thrilled
Sean was thrilled to be chosen to play Peter Pan.

→ over the moon; walking on air

ANTONYM: **sad**

hard

hard (1) ADJECTIVE

An object that is **hard** is very firm and stiff.

firm
The mattress felt much too firm.

solid
They stepped cautiously, trying to stand on solid ground.

stiff
His new jeans felt stiff and uncomfortable.

strong
The champion weightlifter had incredibly strong muscles.

hard (2) ADJECTIVE

If something is **hard** to do, it takes a lot of effort.

exhausting
The hike home in the sun was exhausting.

tiring
Luke doesn't like cycling. He says it's too tiring.

tough
It was a tough climb, but we made it.

hard (3) ADJECTIVE

Hard can mean difficult to understand.

complicated
It was a complicated question but I think I got the answer right.

difficult
Some of the problems we have to deal with are really difficult.

harm VERB

To **harm** means to injure someone or damage something.

damage
The use of too many chemicals can damage the environment.

hurt
It won't hurt her to do a bit of work for a change.

ill-treat
The children were taught never to ill-treat an animal.

injure
He beat down the brambles so that they would not injure anybody.

ruin
"Careless washing could ruin this delicate material," said Amanda.

wound
It was obvious the arrow was meant to wound him.

harsh ADJECTIVE

Harsh conditions are severe, difficult and unpleasant.

cruel
Rain and a cruel wind cut through his clothes and froze him to the bone.

hard
Dickens's stories tell how hard life was in Victorian London.

merciless
Few people survive the merciless conditions of this desert.

severe
A severe winter made things difficult for the farmers.

hate VERB
If you **hate** something, you have a strong feeling of dislike for it.

be sick of
*Mum said she **was sick of** doing the washing-up by herself.*

despise
*I **despise** the way he tried to cheat. It was really underhand.*

detest
*"I really **detest** going to football matches," said Veronica.*

dislike
*Greg **disliked** the way his sister got her way by crying.*

loathe
*"I **loathe** tea," said Mark crossly. "I asked for hot chocolate."*

have (1) VERB
If you **have** something, you own or possess it.

keep
*"Can I **keep** this pen?" asked Tom.*

own
*"Exactly how many books do you **own**?" queried Angus.*

possess
*A good president must **possess** strong leadership skills.*

have (2) VERB
If you **have** something like a good time, you experience it.

experience
*"I **experience** an amazing feeling of excitement," said the skydiver.*

feel
*My sister **felt** great happiness on her wedding day.*

healthy (1) ADJECTIVE
Someone who is **healthy** is well and is not suffering from any illness.

fit
*Grandma keeps **fit** by walking every day.*

in good shape INFORMAL
*Ken has to stay **in good shape** for his job.*

sound
*The doctor said her heart was **sound**.*

strong
*Our football coach is very **strong**.*

well
*I can't go to camp unless I'm **well**.*

ANTONYM: ill

healthy (2) ADJECTIVE
Something that is **healthy** is good for you.

bracing
*What you need is a **bracing** walk.*

good for you
*Greens are **good for you**, so eat them up.*

nourishing
*Our cat still looks skinny though it eats lots of **nourishing** food.*

wholesome
*Mum's cakes are too **wholesome** for me.*

ANTONYM: unhealthy

heap NOUN
A **heap** is a lot of things piled up, usually rather untidily.

mass
*His bed was covered with a **mass** of discarded clothes.*

mound
*Mum sighed at the **mound** of ironing waiting to be done.*

pile
*There was a huge **pile** of books to read.*

stack
*Next to the sink was a **stack** of dirty plates.*

help

help VERB

If you **help** someone, you make things better or easier for them.

assist
The children **assisted** each other with their history project.

give a hand
"Come on," she shouted. "**Give** me **a hand**, can't you?"

improve
If you work a bit harder, it will **improve** your chances.

lend a hand
My brother couldn't manage on his own, so I **lent a hand**.

save
The baby nearly fell over, but I **saved** him.

helpful ADJECTIVE

Someone **helpful** is ready to give assistance or advice.

caring
We've got a **caring** neighbour who feeds the cat when we're away.

friendly
The teachers are always **friendly** if you need anything.

kind
The nurse was very **kind** when I fell and hurt my wrist.

thoughtful
"How **thoughtful** of you," said the king. "I've always wanted one of those!"

willing
Douglas was easily the most **willing** boy in the class.

hesitate VERB

If you **hesitate**, you pause while you are doing something, or before you do it.

delay
The head teacher decided not to **delay**, but to go straight on with his talk.

dither
Rupert **dithered**, trying to think of the right words.

pause
She **paused** and then said, "This applies to all of you."

wait
He **waited** for a moment but nobody offered to help, so he did it himself.

hide (1) VERB

If you **hide** somewhere, you go where you cannot be seen.

lie low
He decided to **lie low** until all the fuss was over.

take cover
They **took cover** in an old shed until the danger was past.

hide (2) VERB

If you **hide** something, you cover it or put it in a place where it can't be seen.

conceal
She **concealed** the scar on her throat with a scarf.

cover
Mum **covered** the hole in the carpet with a rug.

hit (1) VERB

If you **hit** something, you touch it quickly and hard.

beat
*He **beat** the drum as hard as he could.*

clout
*A falling branch **clouted** me on my right shoulder.*

knock
*Laura accidentally **knocked** her head on the doorframe.*

punch
*She tried to **punch** Ben on the nose, but he ducked.*

slap
*Roger's the jolly sort of person who **slaps** you on the back.*

smack
*A twig sprang back and **smacked** Sam in the face.*

strike
*Nista **struck** the ball and it flew over to the boundary.*

stub
*My brother cried when he **stubbed** his toe on the step.*

thump
*"I won't have it!" he shouted, and **thumped** the table.*

whack
*Andrew **whacked** the ball hard back over the net.*

hit (2) VERB

If you **hit** something, you collide with it.

bang
*I **banged** my head on the shelf.*

bump
*Terry fell down and **bumped** his knee.*

bump into
*Ruben couldn't stop in time and **bumped into** the fence.*

crash into
*Freddie skidded on the ice and then **crashed into** a dustbin.*

run into
*Dad **ran into** the back of another car.*

smash into
*A boat **smashed into** the harbour wall.*

hoarse ADJECTIVE

A **hoarse** voice sounds rough.

croaky
*Nina's cold left her too **croaky** to talk for long.*

gruff
*"Dad sounds **gruff**," said Mel, "but he's really nice."*

husky
*"That **husky** voice is just right!" cried the drama teacher.*

rasping
*"My throat's awfully sore," said the dragon in **rasping** tones.*

hold

hold (1) VERB

When you **hold** something, you keep it in your hand or arms.

carry
*Can you **carry** this bag for me, please?*

clasp
*He **clasped** the kitten to him and buried his face in its fur.*

clutch
*Emily **clutched** her mother's hand in sudden panic.*

cradle
*Stuart **cradled** the new baby carefully in his arms.*

embrace
*Dad ran along the platform and **embraced** us both.*

grip
*Gus **gripped** his little brother's hand as they crossed the road.*

hug
*Ellie **hugged** her teddy bear and sang it a song.*

hold (2) VERB

If something **holds** a particular amount of something, it can contain that amount.

accommodate
*The caravan will **accommodate** two adults and four children.*

carry
*Our new car **carries** six people in comfort.*

contain
*That barrel **contains** enough water for hundreds of plants.*

take
*The picnic basket will **take** food for ten.*

hole NOUN

A **hole** is an opening or space in something.

burrow
*A rabbit stuck its head out of a **burrow** just as a fox was passing.*

cave
*There was a large **cave** in the hillside and they couldn't resist a look.*

crack
*Two men were fishing through a **crack** in the ice.*

crater
*Huge **craters** can be seen on the surface of the planet.*

gap
*They peered through a **gap** in the fence and saw a pile of rubbish.*

leak
*Mind the water on the floor. The pipe's got a **leak**.*

pit
*The pirates worked all afternoon, digging a **pit** to hide their treasure.*

pothole
*Marshall hit a **pothole** in the road and came off his bike.*

tear
*Mum groaned when she saw the **tear** in my jeans.*

tunnel
*The rabbit dug a **tunnel** under the fence and escaped.*

honest ADJECTIVE

Someone who is **honest** tells the truth and can be trusted.

law-abiding

Mr Thomson is very **law-abiding**. He always parks carefully.

sincere

My sister said she wanted my **sincere** opinion of her new hairstyle.

trustworthy

Jude's **trustworthy**, so we'll ask her to collect the money.

truthful

The teacher said she only wanted a **truthful** report.

hopeless (1) ADJECTIVE

You say a situation is **hopeless** when it is very bad and you do not think it will get better.

desperate

The tide was coming in and their situation was **desperate**.

futile

He decided his efforts were **futile**.

impossible

Kelly said the whole project was **impossible** and they should give up.

pointless

"This is a **pointless** exercise," said Robin finally.

useless

"Shouting is **useless**," sneered the witch. "Nobody can hear you."

vain

They struggled hard in a **vain** attempt to shift the rock.

hopeless (2) ADJECTIVE

If somebody is **hopeless** at doing something, they cannot do it well.

incompetent

The plumber was **incompetent** and all the pipes leaked.

no good

Grandad's **no good** at dancing, but he doesn't let that stop him.

poor

Uncle Eddie is so **poor** at DIY all his shelves fall down.

useless

She might be **useless** as a cricketer, but she's a brilliant friend.

horrible ADJECTIVE

Someone or something that is **horrible** is awful or unpleasant.

awful

I've got an **awful** headache.

horrid

He was a **horrid** little man with foul-smelling breath.

mean

She played a really **mean** trick on him.

nasty

The crocodile bared its sharp teeth in a **nasty** smile.

unpleasant

The weather was too **unpleasant** for us to play outside.

hot

hot (1) ADJECTIVE

Something or someone that is **hot** has a high temperature.

baking
It was **baking** outdoors so we sat in the shade under a tree.

blazing
The camels trudged across the desert under the **blazing** sun.

boiling
Grandpa hates the cold, so it's always **boiling** in his house.

burning
The nurse laid a cool hand on Christopher's **burning** forehead.

feverish
He felt **feverish** and his throat was sore, so his mum sent for the doctor.

scalding
The water in the bath was **scalding**, so she added cold.

ANTONYM: cold

hot (2) ADJECTIVE

You say food is **hot** if it has a strong spicy taste.

peppery
The meal was a bit too **peppery** for me.

spicy
Dad likes his curries really **spicy**.

ANTONYM: mild

hungry ADJECTIVE

When you are **hungry**, you want to eat.

famished
"Fee, fi, fo, fum!" roared the huge ogre. "I'm **famished**."

peckish
"I expect you're **peckish**," she said, and piled the plate high.

ravenous
We were **ravenous** after our swim.

starving
Starving birds pecked at the seeds we put out in the garden.

hurry VERB

If you **hurry** somewhere, you go there as quickly as you can.

dash
Patch **dashed** off towards home.

fly
Collin heard his dad coming and **flew** to meet him.

get a move on
If we don't **get a move on** we'll be late for the party.

run
She **ran** all the way to school and arrived just before the bell rang.

rush
Adam **rushes** everywhere.

scurry
A mouse **scurried** across the floor and out of the back door.

hurt

hurt (1) VERB

If part of your body **hurts**, you feel pain.

ache
*My tooth has been **aching** all day.*

smart
*Smoke from the bonfire blew in his face and made his eyes **smart**.*

sting
*Tamzin's cut **stung** when she put cream on it.*

tingle
*His leg **tingled** where he'd brushed against the nettles.*

throb
*The music was so loud that his head began to **throb**.*

hurt (2) VERB

If you have been **hurt**, you have been injured.

damage
*The doctor told them Damien's eye was slightly **damaged**.*

harm
*Luckily I wasn't **harmed** when glass in the window broke.*

injure
*A lot of people were **injured** in the motorway accident.*

maim
*If the branch had fallen on him, he could have been **maimed** or killed.*

wound
*I **wounded** my knee when I fell off the bike.*

hurt (3) VERB

To **hurt** someone can mean to upset them.

distress
*You must be careful not to **distress** the new hamster.*

sadden
*It **saddened** Petra to think of her friend moving away.*

torment
*You'd better stop **tormenting** that cat or it will scratch you.*

upset
*Don't say anything to Grandma. It will only **upset** her.*

hurt (4) ADJECTIVE

If you feel **hurt**, you are upset or offended.

distress
*She was **distressed***

grieved
*Peter was **grieved** by his friend's refusal to talk to him.*

insulted
*Atlas was **insulted** when someone said he was feeble.*

offended
*The old lady was **offended** when I tried to help her cross the road.*

upset
*Stefan was **upset** to see the state of his new mountain bike.*

Ii

idea NOUN

If you have an **idea**, you suddenly think of a way of doing something.

brainwave

*Harriet had a sudden **brainwave** and solved the problem.*

plan

*I've thought of a **plan** to get some money.*

scheme

*That's just another of his mad **schemes**.*

suggestion

*The head teacher didn't think much of the **suggestion**.*

ill ADJECTIVE

Someone who is **ill** has something wrong with their health.

ailing

*The king was **ailing**, so the princess played some music to cheer him up.*

queasy

*I always feel **queasy** on boats.*

sick

*Fabio's mum said he was too **sick** to go to school.*

unwell

*The clown came on with a giant ice pack on his head and said he was **unwell**.*

illness NOUN

An **illness** is something like a cold or measles that people can suffer from.

ailment

*His sister's always complaining of some **ailment** or other.*

bug

*Lizzie was off school with a stomach **bug** last week.*

disease

*Polluted water can cause terrible **diseases**.*

imaginary ADJECTIVE

Something that is **imaginary** is not real. It is only in your mind.

dreamlike

*The whole of the afternoon had a **dreamlike** quality.*

fanciful

*Becky is full of **fanciful** tales about having a pet dragon.*

fictitious

*Peter Pan is a **fictitious** character.*

invented

*Nearly all of her so-called adventures are **invented**.*

made-up

*"I don't believe you," said Jim. "I think that is a **made-up** story."*

unreal

*It all felt **unreal**, as if he were in a film.*

important (1) ADJECTIVE

If someone says something is **important**, they mean it matters a lot.

basic
Basic equipment for camping includes a good tent.

big
*The next **big** event is the school play.*

essential
*Water is **essential** for all living things.*

main
*"The **main** thing is that you all enjoy yourselves," said the dance teacher.*

major
*Exercise is a **major** part of staying healthy.*

necessary
*Fitness and common sense are **necessary** qualities for a good rock climber.*

serious
*At the last minute they discovered a **serious** flaw in their plan.*

special
*Mum and Dad are celebrating another **special** anniversary.*

important (2) ADJECTIVE

Someone who is **important** has a lot of power in a particular group.

famous
*We're going to meet a **famous** film star.*

high-ranking
*His dad's a **high-ranking** police officer.*

leading
*Esmeralda had a **leading** part in the school play.*

powerful
*The President of the United States is in a **powerful** position.*

impressive ADJECTIVE

If something is **impressive**, people admire it, usually because it is large or important.

awe-inspiring
*Edmund gazed up at the mountain. It was **awe-inspiring**.*

grand
*They came upon a huge house with a **grand** garden.*

great
*I stared at the **great** stone statue in the hotel courtyard.*

magnificent
*The trees were **magnificent**. They were the tallest he'd ever seen.*

increase VERB

If something **increases**, it becomes greater.

expand
*As he became older his waistline **expanded** alarmingly.*

extend
*The school is hoping to **extend** the size of the playing fields.*

grow
*The number of students at the school is expected to **grow** next year.*

multiply
*These germs can spread easily and **multiply** rapidly.*

rise
*The teacher was pleased that the number of children using the library had **risen**.*

ANTONYM: decrease

informal

informal ADJECTIVE

Informal means relaxed and casual.

casual
*On Friday we can wear **casual** clothes to school.*

easy
*Our doctor has a very **easy** manner.*

friendly
*It was just a **friendly** match.*

natural
*He wasn't at all pompous and just chatted in a **natural** way.*

relaxed
*It was a very **relaxed** interview.*

information NOUN

If someone gives you **information** about something, they tell you about it.

facts
*The police said they had several leads in the case, but needed more **facts**.*

material
*You'll find plenty of **material** on this subject in the library.*

news
*The soldier's friends and family were anxiously awaiting **news**.*

notice
*We'll get plenty of **notice** nearer the time.*

word
*The head teacher said he'd received **word** that a famous author was coming.*

insect NOUN

An **insect** is a small animal with six legs. It usually has wings.

SOME INSECTS:
ant
bee
beetle
butterfly
dragonfly
fly
grasshopper
ladybird
wasp

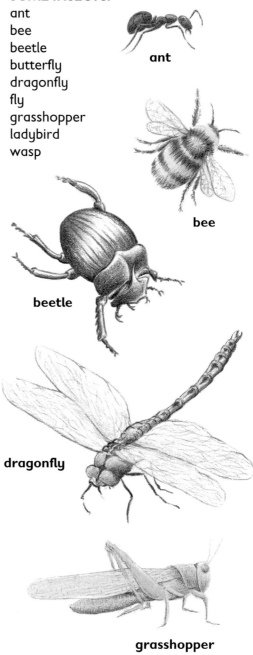

ant

bee

beetle

dragonfly

grasshopper

ladybird

interesting ADJECTIVE

If something is **interesting**, it attracts or holds your attention.

amazing
"That is an **amazing** firework display," said Toni.

amusing
His uncle knows lots of **amusing** stories about animals.

entertaining
The girls watched an **entertaining** programme on the television.

exciting
Andy leads an **exciting** life as an explorer.

fascinating
Grandma said she found my polar bear story **fascinating**.

gripping
The plot was so **gripping** George couldn't put the book down.

intriguing
The police found the mystery **intriguing**.

unusual
The dog dug up an **unusual** object.

invent VERB

If someone **invents** something such as a machine, they are the first person to think of it.

come up with
His mum asked him to **come up with** a name for her shop.

create
I'd like to **create** a robot to do my homework and tidy my room.

design
They were asked to **design** a new way of packing eggs.

devise
Billy tried to **devise** a way of opening the door without getting up.

plan
We **planned** a different layout for the new train set.

think up
It's not easy to **think up** something completely new.

invisible ADJECTIVE

If something is **invisible**, it cannot be seen.

concealed
The conjuror made sure everything was **concealed** ready for the tricks.

disguised
Chameleons can become **disguised** when they change colour.

hidden
A leopard was **hidden** in the dappled shade of the trees.

microscopic
Out there is a whole world of things that are **microscopic**.

ANTONYM: visible

a
b
c
d
e
f
g
h
Ii
j
k
l
m
n
o
p
q
r
s
t
u
v
w
x
y
z

a
b
c
d
e
f
g
h
i
Jj
k
l
m
n
o
p
q
r
s
t
u
v
w
x
y
z

Jj

jagged ADJECTIVE

Something **jagged** has an uneven edge with sharp points on it.

broken
The wall was topped with **broken** glass.

rough
Steven tore his sleeve on the **rough** edge of a rock.

uneven
She trimmed the photo rapidly with careless, **uneven** cuts.

jam VERB

If you **jam** something in somewhere, you push it there roughly.

cram
In a fury, the witch **crammed** her hat on her head and strode out of the door.

pack
Aziz **packed** more and more clothes into the case until it was bursting.

squeeze
We couldn't see how they were going to **squeeze** us all in.

jealous ADJECTIVE

Someone who is **jealous** feels upset because someone else has what they want.

envious
Lizzie was always **envious** of her big sister's new clothes.

resentful
Charles was **resentful** of all the attention people paid his baby brother.

upset
Sandra will be **upset** if she doesn't get a present too.

jet NOUN

A **jet** is a stream of liquid or gas forced out under pressure.

fountain
The firework exploded in a **fountain** of coloured lights.

gush
They had to leap back to avoid the sudden **gush** from the tap.

spray
Dad sent a **spray** of water over the car to clean it.

spurt
There was a small **spurt** of blood when Debbie cut her finger.

squirt
A **squirt** of ink from the fountain pen went across his homework.

jewel NOUN

A **jewel** is a precious stone, such as a diamond or a ruby, used to make things like rings and necklaces.

gem
Her ring had a single **gem** set in silver.

gemstone
The duchess wore a tiara sparkling with rare **gemstones**.

ornament
King Ralph wore several valuable **ornaments** around his neck.

precious stone
Her earrings twinkled with **precious stones**.

rock
The singer wore **rocks** the size of marbles on his fingers.

stone
"What a beautiful **stone**," gushed Sandra. "Was it expensive?"

job (1) NOUN

A **job** is the work that someone does to earn money.

employment
Dad says the new building will bring plenty of employment.

occupation
Firefighting is a dangerous occupation.

work
"What work does your mum do?" asked Sebastian casually.

job (2) NOUN

A **job** can be anything that has to be done.

chore
I have to do chores like making my bed before I go to school.

errand
Ron had a few errands to do before he met his friends.

task
Our first task was to make a timetable.

SOME JOBS PEOPLE DO:

actor	electrician	optician
architect	engineer	plumber
artist	farmer	police officer
builder	firefighter	postman/woman
chemist	lawyer	scientist
cook	librarian	teacher
dentist	musician	vet
designer	nurse	writer
doctor		

musician

firefighter

artist

vet

farmer

join

join (1) VERB

If you **join** a club or organization, you become a member of it.

become a member of
I've **become a member of** the local library.

enlist in
My brother is planning to **enlist in** the army when he finishes school.

enrol in
Jessie wanted to **enrol in** the dancing class.

join (2) VERB

To **join** can mean to fasten two things together.

attach
He **attached** the pages with a clip.

connect
Dad tried to **connect** two pipes, but they came unstuck.

fix
They had to **fix** the sides of the box with adhesive tape.

stick
Abdul **stuck** the wings on with glue.

tie
Clare **tied** the ends of the ribbon in a bow.

join (3) VERB

When things **join**, they come together.

border on
Philomena's garden **borders on** the most beautiful countryside.

combine
This clever play manages to **combine** terror with comedy.

come together
The two footpaths **came together** in a sunlit clearing.

meet
We arranged to **meet** the others at the railway station.

reach
When they **reached** the main road they found it heavy with traffic.

journey NOUN

If you go on a **journey**, you travel from one place to another.

drive
Dad took us on a **drive** to the seaside.

excursion
The **excursion** was by coach.

expedition
John and Patrick planned an **expedition** to the island.

flight
It is a very long **flight** from London to Sydney.

hike
The **hike** took them deep into the snow-covered mountains.

ride
Lee enjoyed her **ride** to Gran's house.

tour
My brother wants to go on a **tour** to see all the Welsh castles.

trek
They found themselves on an exhausting **trek** through the forest.

trip
The **trip** should have been fun, but it turned out to be rather boring.

voyage
It was a long **voyage**, and Jeremy soon became seasick.

walk
We were looking forward to our five-mile **walk** in the countryside.

judge VERB

If you **judge** someone or something, you form an opinion about them.

appreciate
*You have to know something about art to **appreciate** these paintings.*

assess
*The teacher asked us to **assess** each other's science project.*

consider
*Everyone in the village **considers** Dad's cooking to be fantastic.*

decide
*At the dog show they **decided** Fifi the French poodle should win top prize.*

evaluate
*Three teachers sat on the platform **evaluating** the dancers' performances.*

rate
*The review **rated** Holly's violin playing as exceptional for her age.*

rule
*Finally, the head teacher **ruled** that Chris was the winner.*

sized up
*Mum **sized up** the situation very quickly and sent us both to bed.*

juice NOUN

Juice is the liquid that comes from fruit such as oranges when you squeeze them.

fluid
*He cut the orange in half and **fluid** ran onto the table.*

liquid
*As she squeezed the fruit, drops of **liquid** fell into the cake mixture.*

jump VERB

When you **jump**, you spring off the ground using your leg muscles.

bounce
*Gareth **bounced** up and hit the ball in the air.*

bound
*The kangaroo **bounded** across the ground at great speed.*

hop
*A rabbit **hopped** away in front of them.*

leap
*Jamil watched squirrels **leaping** through the trees.*

pounce
*Our cat likes to **pounce** on mice, but she usually misses.*

skip
*Julia **skipped** up and down when her team scored a goal.*

spring
*He **sprang** up at once and offered to help.*

vault
*Jessie **vaulted** over the gate as the dog raced towards her.*

a
b
c
d
e
f
g
h
i
Jj
k
l
m
n
o
p
q
r
s
t
u
v
w
x
y
z

keen

keen ADJECTIVE

Someone who is **keen** to do something wants to do it very much.

anxious
Ellie was **anxious** to show how well she could cope.

avid
He was an **avid** supporter of the local football team.

eager
The whole class was **eager** to go on the outing to the zoo.

enthusiastic
Terry only wants people in his team who are **enthusiastic**.

keep (1) VERB

If you **keep** something, you store it.

put
Mum **puts** the house keys in a special box so they don't get lost.

store
Mr Jones **stores** apples in his shed.

stow
I **stow** my toys in the cupboard.

keep (2) VERB

If you **keep** something, you have it and look after it.

care for
The wildlife centre **cares for** otters here.

look after
That lady **looks after** cats that need a good home.

run
His dad **runs** a small sweetshop not far from here.

keep (3) VERB

If you **keep** doing something, you do it over and over again.

carry on
The teacher told him to stop, but he **carried on** doing it.

go on
Aunt Rudy says she'll **go on** working here until she retires.

kill VERB

To **kill** someone or something means to make them die.

assassinate
Powerful people, such as presidents, are sometimes **assassinated**.

destroy
The dog had to be **destroyed** because it was so vicious.

execute
King Charles I was **executed**.

exterminate
Dad has been trying to **exterminate** the slugs in our garden.

murder
To **murder** someone is a terrible crime.

put to sleep
Jade was upset when her cat was so ill it had to be **put to sleep**.

slaughter
All animals affected by the disease had to be **slaughtered**.

slay
The knight set out at once to **slay** the terrifying dragon.

kind (1) ADJECTIVE

Someone who is **kind** behaves in a gentle, caring way.

friendly
That old lady's quite friendly. She always throws our ball back.

gentle
I like my dentist. He is very gentle.

helpful
The librarian's helpful when you can't find a book.

thoughtful
"It was thoughtful of you to bring flowers," she said.

understanding
Our teacher's very understanding if you don't feel well.

kind (2) NOUN

If you talk about a **kind** of object, you mean a sort of object.

brand
What brand of cornflakes do you have?

sort
John has got all sorts of games.

type
"I really like this type of food," said Uncle Henry.

know (1) VERB

If you **know** a fact, you have it in your mind and don't need to learn it.

be certain of
"I am certain of one thing," said Mum. "You're going to bed now."

be sure of
David was sure of the answer.

realize
They suddenly realized that they had been tricked.

see
You must see that your plan won't work.

understand
At last he understood exactly what the teacher meant.

know (2) VERB

If you **know** somebody, you have met them before.

identify
James identified the man by his strange, curly moustache.

recognize
I would recognize him anywhere.

knowledge NOUN

Knowledge is the information and understanding that you have.

education
Education has helped him get the job he really wanted.

facts
Don't make up your mind about this until you have enough facts.

information
Police say they now have all the information they need to solve the case.

learning
The professor was a man of great learning who could talk about anything.

wisdom
People who are thoughtful usually gain wisdom as they grow older.

a
b
c
d
e
f
g
h
i
j
Kk
l
m
n
o
p
q
r
s
t
u
v
w
x
y
z

Ll

land (1) NOUN

Land is the part of the world that is solid, dry ground.

earth
*The **earth** was too dry and farmers were desperate for rain.*

ground
*After the rain, the **ground** was quickly covered with bright green shoots.*

soil
*He dug lots of compost into the **soil** to help the plants grow.*

land (2) NOUN

A **land** is a region or country.

country
*"Mexico is a very large **country** in Central America," said the teacher.*

nation
*Leaders of friendly **nations** meet to discuss important things.*

region
*Different **regions** of the world have their own climates.*

territory
*Wars are sometimes fought about the boundaries of **territory**.*

land (3) VERB

When a bird or aircraft **lands**, it comes down on to land or water.

alight
*A blackbird **alighted** on a branch above their heads.*

arrive
*The plane was due to **arrive** in Paris in the late afternoon.*

come down
*They **came down** with hardly a bump, and the journey was over.*

come to rest
*Wild geese skimmed above the lake and **came to rest** close to the hide.*

touch down
*"We shall be **touching down** in a few minutes," said the pilot as the jumbo jet began its descent.*

last (1) ADJECTIVE

If something happens **last**, it happens after everything else.

closing
*The **closing** bars of the music sounded loud and triumphant.*

concluding
*I almost forgot to read out the **concluding** paragraph of my talk.*

final
*Charlotte has had a **final** warning about her homework and she is determined to do better next time.*

ANTONYM: **first**

last (2) VERB

If something **lasts**, it continues to exist or happen.

carry on
*His speech seemed to **carry on** forever.*

continue
*They were hoping Auntie Anne's good mood would **continue**.*

remain
*The castle has **remained** in reasonable condition for centuries.*

survive
*We needed the car to **survive** at least until the holiday was over.*

laugh VERB

When you **laugh**, you make a sound that shows you think something is funny.

cackle
*"That's really funny," **cackled** the witch.*

giggle
*The two children **giggled** at each other.*

snigger
*The others **sniggered** when they saw my new jumper.*

→ fall about laughing; laugh your head off; roar with laughter; split your sides

law NOUN

A **law** is a rule that is made by the government.

code
*Drivers are expected to follow strict **codes** of behaviour on the road.*

regulation
*There are **regulations** to control the hours pilots spend flying.*

rule
*An important **rule** is that children go to school regularly.*

lay VERB

If you **lay** something somewhere, you put it there carefully.

place
*They collected the papers and **placed** them on her desk.*

put
*"Just **put** it down anywhere on the table," she said.*

set down
*He **set down** the book in front of her.*

spread
*Dad **spread** a rug on the damp grass.*

layer NOUN

A **layer** is a single thickness of something that lies on top of or underneath something else.

blanket
*A **blanket** of fog hid the landscape.*

coat
*The decorator said the door needed another **coat** of paint.*

coating
*Mum added a thick **coating** of icing sugar to the cake.*

film
*Nothing had disturbed the **film** of dust on the mantelpiece.*

sheet
*The pond was covered with a **sheet** of ice.*

leak NOUN

A **leak** is a hole that lets gas or liquid escape.

chink
*Gas was escaping through a small **chink**.*

crack
*The roots of a tree had caused a **crack** in the waste pipe.*

hole
*Water seeped through several small **holes** in the swimming pool.*

puncture
*She watched the tyre go flat as air hissed from the **puncture**.*

leave VERB

When you **leave** a person or place, you go away from them.

abandon
*One of the sheep **abandoned** its lamb.*

desert
*Our cat would never **desert** her kittens.*

go
*Let's **go** as soon as the play is over.*

resign
*Mum's going to **resign** her position.*

set off
*They **set off** in a frantic rush.*

level ADJECTIVE

A surface that is **level** is smooth, flat and parallel to the ground.

even
*Nothing was allowed to spoil the **even** appearance of the lawn.*

flat
*Shannon needed somewhere **flat** to leave her artwork.*

horizontal
*Every **horizontal** surface held books and piles of papers.*

smooth
*At last the wood was **smooth** and ready to make into a table.*

lie (1) VERB

To **lie** somewhere means to rest there horizontally.

lounge
*My brother just **lounges** about all day.*

recline
*Auntie Hilary **reclined** in a deckchair with a book on her lap.*

rest
*Sebastian wanted to **rest** on the bench after the game of tennis.*

sprawl
*Alexander **sprawled** in the chair with his eyes closed.*

stretch out
*The dog **stretched out** on the floor and went to sleep.*

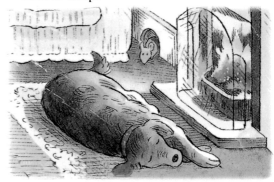

lie (2) VERB

To **lie** means to say something that is not true.

bluff
*Don't worry about it. He's **bluffing**.*

fib
*She often **fibs** to get out of trouble.*

light (1) ADJECTIVE

A place that is **light** is bright because of the sun or the use of lamps.

airy
*She showed them into a large, **airy** room.*

bright
*It was much **brighter** outside.*

well-lit
*Sue's room was quite small but **well-lit**.*

light (2) ADJECTIVE

A **light** object does not weigh much.

delicate

*Chelsea wore a **delicate**, long-sleeved dress to the party.*

flimsy

*The fairy's wings were **flimsy** and see-through.*

light (3) VERB

To **light** a fire means to make it start burning.

catch fire

*The wood was damp and wouldn't **catch fire** immediately.*

ignite

*Dad **ignited** the rocket and stood well back with the rest of us.*

light (4) ADJECTIVE

A **light** colour is pale.

fair

*Rhiannon's **fair** skin burned very easily in the sun.*

pale

*The sky was a **pale** blue.*

pastel

*My shirt was a **pastel** yellow colour.*

like VERB

If you **like** someone or something, you find them pleasant.

adore

*Sophie **adores** the new puppies.*

enjoy

*What sorts of films do you **enjoy**?*

love

*Our parrot **loves** ginger biscuits.*

→ be crazy about; be mad about

little ADJECTIVE

Someone or something that is **little** is small in size.

brief

*"That skirt is too **brief** to wear outside," said Mum.*

narrow

*A **narrow** path led down through the trees to the river.*

small

*He gave her a **small** bite of his chocolate and nut bar.*

tiny

*The baby wore a **tiny** bracelet on her wrist.*

young

*My brother's only **young**. That's why he doesn't understand.*

lively ADJECTIVE

Someone who is **lively** is cheerful and full of energy.

active

*The baby's always **active** when he's just had a sleep.*

chirpy

*Her grandmother sounded **chirpy** after her visit to the theatre.*

energetic

*Ed felt really **energetic** during the first football game of the season.*

frisky

*Rover grew **frisky** as soon as he saw the ducks on the lake.*

perky

*"He looks much **perkier** today," said the doctor. "Back to school tomorrow!"*

a
b
c
d
e
f
g
h
i
j
k
Ll
m
n
o
p
q
r
s
t
u
v
w
x
y
z

lonely

lonely (1) ADJECTIVE

Someone who is **lonely** is unhappy because they are on their own, or do not have any friends.

alone
*You can sometimes feel **alone**, even when you are in a crowd.*

forlorn
*Francesco was **forlorn** when his big brother left home.*

friendless
*At first he felt **friendless** at his new school.*

lonesome
*Fluffy is **lonesome** without her kittens.*

unhappy
*The dog seems **unhappy** now Kim's at school all day.*

lonely (2) ADJECTIVE

A **lonely** place is away from towns and is not visited by many people.

isolated
*They stayed in an **isolated** cottage on the edge of a lake.*

remote
*The farmer's sheep grazed quietly on a **remote** hillside.*

secluded
*They found a **secluded** spot far away from the road.*

solitary
*Grandpa grew up in a **solitary** farm with no running water.*

uninhabited
*Through the telescope they saw a small, **uninhabited** island.*

→ off the beaten track; out-of-the-way

look (1) VERB

If you **look** in a particular direction, you turn your eyes that way.

gaze
*She **gazed** at the beautiful countryside around her.*

glance
*Anoop **glanced** across at her, then smiled and waved.*

peep
*Peter **peeped** in through the window.*

peer
*Grandma **peered** at the badge on my denim jacket.*

stare
*Alice **stared** at the White Rabbit as he turned away.*

watch
*From the cliff top they **watched** as men unloaded a small boat.*

look (2) VERB

How someone **looks** is how they appear or seem to be.

appear
*When William arrived at school, he **appeared** anxious.*

seem
*Dad **seemed** pleased about something, but he wouldn't tell us what.*

seem to be
*The baby **seems to be** happier when I'm there to play with her.*

loud ADJECTIVE

A **loud** sound is one that makes a lot of noise.

deafening
*There was a **deafening** bang as the firework went off.*

harsh
*The raven's cries were **harsh** and unpleasant to listen to.*

noisy
*Mum complained that we were all being too **noisy**.*

piercing
*Rosie gave a **piercing** shriek when she saw the spider.*

shrill
*The old lady's voice was **shrill** with anger.*

thunderous
*One of the lions gave a **thunderous** roar.*

→ ear-piercing; ear-splitting

ANTONYM: quiet

love (1) VERB

If you **love** someone, you have strong feelings of affection for them.

adore
*My brother **adores** his new girlfriend.*

be fond of
*Christopher Robin **was fond of** Pooh Bear.*

worship
*Georgina really **worships** her dad.*

ANTONYM: hate

love (2) VERB

If you **love** something, you like it very much.

enjoy
*Thomas **enjoys** reading.*

like
*I **like** any kind of pasta.*

lump (1) NOUN

A **lump** is a piece of something solid.

ball
*She took a **ball** of modelling clay and began to work.*

cake
*The new **cake** of soap smelled of roses.*

chunk
*One of the ducks gobbled a **chunk** of stale bread.*

piece
*A mysterious **piece** of rock suddenly appeared on the path.*

wedge
*Darcy helped himself to a generous **wedge** of cheese.*

lump (2) NOUN

A **lump** can be a bump on the surface of something.

bulge
*He tried to pretend he wasn't eating anything, but there was a suspicious **bulge** in his cheek.*

bump
*The road was terrible but they tried to avoid the worst of the **bumps**.*

swelling
*Thomas had a **swelling** over one eye after the fight.*

Mm

magic NOUN

In stories, **magic** is the thing that makes impossible things happen.

SOME KINDS OF MAGIC:

conjuring	spells
enchantment	trickery
hocus-pocus	witchcraft
illusion	wizardry

magical ADJECTIVE

Something that is **magical** is wonderful and exciting.

fascinating
The magician wore a cloak covered in ***fascinating*** *designs.*

marvellous
We had a ***marvellous*** *tree completely covered in decorations.*

spellbinding
The lights in the city were ***spellbinding***.

main ADJECTIVE

The **main** part of something is the most important part.

basic
Remember, the ***basic*** *requirement for a singer is talent.*

chief
He outlined the ***chief*** *things he wanted to cover during the lesson.*

essential
"Grass and hay are the ***essential*** *foods for our cows," said the farmer.*

leading
The ***leading*** *actress in the film is famous in Japan.*

major
The ***major*** *reason for Alison's success is hard work.*

make (1) VERB

If you **make** something new, you use your skill to shape it or put it together.

assemble
My model aircraft was quite difficult to ***assemble***.

build
The third little pig ***built*** *his house of bricks.*

form
Oliver ***formed*** *a cat out of clay.*

invent
My dad's trying to ***invent*** *a new kind of mini camera.*

put together
They ***put together*** *all the scenery for the train set.*

make (2) VERB

If you **make** someone do something, you force them to do it.

force
She didn't want to hand over her money but the highwayman ***forced*** *her.*

order
The soldiers were ***ordered*** *to retreat.*

mammal NOUN

A **mammal** is a warm-blooded animal. Female mammals give birth to live babies. They feed their babies with milk from their own bodies.

FARM MAMMALS:
cow
goat
horse
pig
sheep

cow

horse

pig

MAMMALS THAT LIVE IN OR NEAR WATER:
dolphin
hippopotamus
otter
seal
walrus
whale

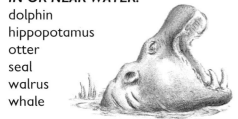

hippopotamus

walrus

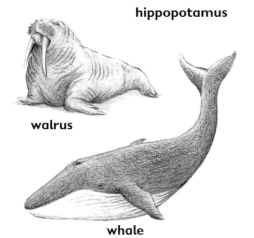

whale

PET MAMMALS:
cat
dog
gerbil
guinea pig
hamster
mouse
rat

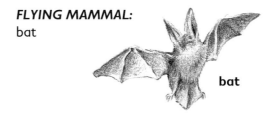

gerbil

guinea pig

FLYING MAMMAL:
bat

bat

WILD MAMMALS:

badger	giraffe	monkey
bear	hare	rabbit
chimpanzee	hedgehog	rhinoceros
deer	kangaroo	squirrel
elephant	koala	tiger
fox	lion	zebra

bear

elephant

SMALLEST MAMMAL:
pygmy shrew (80 mm including tail)

LARGEST MAMMAL:
blue whale (33 m long)

Mm

manage VERB

Someone who **manages** an organization is in charge of it.

be in charge of
"I demand to see whoever is in charge of this restaurant," said the customer.

command
Mr Pecksniff commands a large department in the store.

control
Our teacher controls the class without raising her voice.

direct
The lights broke down and police had to direct the traffic.

look after
Mum said she would look after the games if somebody else did the food.

run
Our local school needs somebody to run the library.

mark NOUN

A **mark** is a small stain on something.

blot
A blot appeared mysteriously on Grace's maths work.

smear
Tony washed his hands but there was still a smear on his face.

smudge
Becky nearly wept when she found a smudge on her drawing.

spot
"Don't worry," said the teacher. "It's only a tiny spot."

stain
There was a damp stain on the wallpaper where the rain had come in.

meal NOUN

A **meal** is food that people eat, usually at set times during the day.

barbecue
It was a lovely evening, so they had a barbecue on the beach.

buffet
Mum arranged a buffet so that people could help themselves.

feast
We pitched our tent in the garden and had a late-night feast.

picnic
For my birthday, we had a lovely picnic beside the river.

snack
Halfway through the morning Toby decided he needed a snack.

mean (1) VERB

If you ask what something **means**, you want it explained to you.

indicates
"That sign indicates no right turn," said the police officer.

say
Can't you read? That sign says you mustn't walk on the grass.

show
The flashing light shows the battery is low.

stand for
What does that symbol stand for?

mean (2) ADJECTIVE

Someone who is **mean** does not like spending money or sharing.

miserly
Scrooge was a miserly person.

selfish
Matt's really selfish. He wouldn't give me any of his sweets.

stingy
Some parents are quite stingy when it comes to pocket money.

mean (3) VERB

If you **mean** to do something, you intend to do it.

aim
*What do you **aim** to do when you grow up?*

intend
*If you **intend** to be prime minister, you'll have to work harder.*

plan
*I **planned** to jump out and surprise him, but it didn't work.*

propose
*"How do you **propose** to sort out this mess?" demanded his mum.*

meet VERB

If you **meet** someone, you go to the same place at the same time as they do.

come across
*We first **came across** her at a disco.*

come upon
*They were walking in the mountains when they **came upon** a troll.*

encounter
*A hermit lives in this wood, but you are not likely to **encounter** him.*

run across
*"You'll never guess who I **ran across** yesterday," said Joe.*

run into
*If we go this way we might **run into** that big dog.*

meeting NOUN

A **meeting** is when a group of people meet to talk about particular things.

audience
*Angry villagers demanded an urgent **audience** with the king.*

conference
*Mr Wilson-Brown is away at a **conference** of head teachers.*

gathering
*Outside the school, a **gathering** of parents discussed the new rules.*

get-together
*Students who were leaving suggested a **get-together** the following year.*

mend VERB

If you **mend** something that is broken or does not work, you put it right so that it can be used again.

cure
*"I know how to **cure** a broken heart," said the fairy.*

darn
*Grandma says she used to **darn** Grandpa's socks to make them last.*

fix
*Harry **fixed** the wonky saddle on his bike.*

patch
*My sister **patched** her jeans with a bright red square.*

repair
*The radio was quite easy to **repair**.*

mess

mess (1) NOUN

If you say something is a **mess**, you mean it is very untidy.

chaos Say "**kay-**oss"
She screamed at the **chaos** she found in the kitchen. There was flour everywhere.

clutter
Dad said if I didn't sort out the **clutter**, he'd do it for me.

disorder
It took a long time to get the **disorder** tidied up, but finally everything was back in the right place.

jumble
"Look at that **jumble** of books," said Mum. "Why is it on the floor?"

litter
There was **litter** everywhere.

shambles
After the party the room was a **shambles**.

mess (2) NOUN

If you are in a **mess**, you are in a situation where there are a lot of problems.

fix
The ruby slippers helped Dorothy out of her **fix**.

jam
David was in a **jam** with his maths homework and needed help.

pickle
The wizard got in a **pickle** with his spell.

→ fine kettle of fish

method NOUN

A **method** is a particular way of doing something.

approach
I think a different **approach** might work a bit better.

manner
Seahorses have an unusual **manner** of giving birth.

plan
Before they began work he explained his **plan** carefully.

system
Barbara has a special **system** for dealing with the mail.

technique
"There is a simple **technique** for sorting out greenfly," said Percy.

way
If you know a better **way** then tell me now.

middle NOUN

The **middle** of something is the part furthest from the edges.

centre
The cat sat in the **centre** of the flowerbed.

heart
The **heart** of the old tree was hollow.

midpoint
By the **midpoint** of the race she was beginning to tire.

thick
William always liked to be in the **thick** of the battle.

mild ADJECTIVE

Someone or something **mild** is gentle and does no harm.

gentle
*The male gorilla had a very **gentle** nature.*

kind
*The witch's tones were **kind**, but they still didn't trust her.*

meek
*"I'm sorry," she said in a **meek** voice. "I didn't mean to hurt you."*

placid
*My great-grandfather has the same **placid** reaction to almost everything.*

pleasant
*She made a **pleasant** comment as she let them through.*

mind (1) NOUN

Your **mind** is your ability to think, together with your memory and all the thoughts you have.

brain
*"I can't get my **brain** round this problem," said Uncle Eddie.*

head
*Emma had plenty of ideas in her **head**. She just needed to transfer them to paper.*

mind (2) VERB

If you **mind** somebody or something, you look after them.

guard
*We let the dog **guard** our ball when we went shopping.*

keep an eye on
*"Please **keep an eye on** my gold," breathed the dragon.*

look after
*Her aunt **looked after** her for the day while her parents were at work.*

take care of
*Caspar the clown **took care of** the performing fleas.*

mind (3) VERB

If you **mind** about something, it worries you or makes you angry.

be bothered
*Daniel **was bothered** about changing schools at the end of the year.*

care
*"I don't **care**," said Jessie. "I've got lots of other friends."*

object to
*The unicorn **objected to** sharing the field with ordinary horses.*

misery NOUN

Misery is great unhappiness.

despair
*Mr Jones was full of **despair** when he lost his job.*

grief
*The swan showed signs of **grief** when its mate died.*

sadness
*We tried to discover the reason for the little boy's **sadness**.*

sorrow
*"Such dreadful **sorrow** is hard to bear," said the wizard.*

unhappiness
*Luckily, her **unhappiness** did not last for more than a day.*

ANTONYM: joy

a
b
c
d
e
f
g
h
i
j
k
l
Mm
n
o
p
q
r
s
t
u
v
w
x
y
z

miss

miss VERB

If you **miss** somebody, you are lonely without them.

feel the loss of
Natalie **felt the loss of** her friend when his family moved.

pine for
Our dog **pined for** my dad while he was away working.

mistake NOUN

A **mistake** is something that is done wrong.

blunder
Tom made a number of **blunders** in the spelling test.

error
"That's excellent," said the teacher. "There are no **errors** at all."

oversight
The king's **oversight** was to forget to invite a fairy godmother.

slip
I only made two small **slips**, but it was enough to make Mum suspicious.

misty ADJECTIVE

If it is **misty**, there are lots of tiny drops of water in the air, and you cannot see very far.

blurred
His eyes were full of tears and everything looked **blurred**.

dim
In the early morning, they watched the **dim** outline of trees becoming clearer.

faint
A **faint** glimmer shone through the clouds.

hazy
The **hazy** sunshine promised a hot day.

indistinct
The figures behind the fountain were **indistinct**, but even through the spray they seemed familiar.

mix VERB

If you **mix** things, you stir them or put them together.

blend
The witch **blended** everything carefully.

combine
If you **combine** blue and yellow you will get green.

mingle
Mum was having a job getting the guests to **mingle** properly.

put together
Holly **put together** flour and water to make a paste.

stir together
Stir together the butter, sugar and eggs in a bowl.

monster NOUN

A **monster** is an imaginary creature that is large and terrifying.

bogey-man
I don't believe in **bogey-men**.

giant
Jack climbed the beanstalk and found a hungry **giant**.

ogre
"You must tell me," said the **ogre**, "why nobody likes me."

troll
A family of **trolls** was having a picnic in the mountains.

move (1) VERB

To **move** means to go to a different place or position.

dart
*A mouse **darted** out from a hole under the door.*

fly
*The bird **flew** away as soon as it saw the farmyard cat.*

gallop
*A ghostly horse **galloped** through the dark forest.*

shoot
*Josephine **shot** across the room to save a falling vase.*

shuffle
*An old man was **shuffling** painfully down the street.*

slither
*Marcus lifted a stone and a small snake **slithered** out.*

stir
*Sam **stirred** uneasily in his sleep.*

totter
*The baby **tottered** a few yards and sat down suddenly.*

tremble
*Leaves **trembled** in the breeze.*

walk
*Jake **walked** slowly across the classroom.*

zoom
*The sports car **zoomed** down the road at great speed.*

move (2) VERB

To **move** something means to change its place or position.

bring
*"Could you **bring** that little table nearer to me?" asked Gran.*

carry
*Martin **carried** the television upstairs.*

disturb
*The professor would not let anyone **disturb** his papers.*

drag
*Dad **dragged** a huge bag of potatoes into the shed.*

fling
*Luke **flung** my jacket off his bed.*

pull
*Ben **pulled** the lever towards him.*

push
*A toddler was trying to **push** her buggy along the pavement.*

take
*"Please **take** those disgusting socks away from me!" exclaimed Jane.*

move (3) VERB

If you **move**, you change where you are living.

migrate
*Some birds **migrate** thousands of miles every year.*

move house
*They **move house** fairly frequently when their mum changes her job.*

music

a
b
c
d
e
f
g
h
i
j
k
l

Mm

n
o
p
q
r
s
t
u
v
w
x
y
z

music NOUN

Music is a pattern of sounds made by people singing or playing instruments.

KINDS OF MUSIC:

classical	pop
country	rap
folk	reggae
jazz	rock
opera	soul

KINDS OF SONGS:

anthem	lullaby
ballad	nursery rhyme
carol	pop song
chant	rap
folk song	round
hymn	

MUSICAL INSTRUMENTS:

bagpipes	guitar	saxophone
banjo	harmonica	sitar
cello	harp	tambourine
clarinet	horn	triangle
didgeridoo	keyboard	trumpet
double bass	oboe	trumpet
drum	piano	violin
flute	recorder	xylophone

drum

flute

guitar

harp

keyboard

mysterious (1) ADJECTIVE

Something that is **mysterious** is strange and puzzling.

baffling
Aunt Alice found the disappearance of the cakes baffling.

curious
"What a curious feeling!" said Alice as she began to shrink.

eerie
The house was dark and eerie and full of strange sounds.

ghostly
A tall ghostly figure floated silently across the terrace.

magical
Deep in the centre of the forest was a magical waterfall.

mystifying
A mystifying sound came from beneath the floorboards.

strange
The wizard wore a dark cloak covered in strange designs.

weird
Suddenly the boys came upon a weird door in the wall.

mysterious (2) ADJECTIVE

If someone is being **mysterious**, they are secretive about something.

furtive
A furtive smile appeared on Jasper's face when he worked out the answer.

puzzling
Sarah was very interested in the men's puzzling behaviour.

secretive
Seth was being surprisingly secretive about his plans.

mystery NOUN

A **mystery** is something strange that cannot be explained.

problem
The boys were determined to solve the problem of the curious footprint.

puzzle
It took them a week to find an answer to the puzzle.

question
"The question is," said the detective, "how did the thief get in?"

riddle
The police were baffled by the riddle of the locked room.

secret
Strange writing told of a secret that could never be known.

a
b
c
d
e
f
g
h
i
j
k
l
m
Nn
o
p
q
r
s
t
u
v
w
x
y
z

Nn

nasty ADJECTIVE

Something or someone **nasty** is very unpleasant.

disgusting
The inside of Tom's trainers smelled really **disgusting**.

horrible
My sister had a **horrible** rash when she caught measles.

mean
Scrooge was a very **mean** person.

stormy
Lifeboat crew often have to go out in **stormy** weather.

unpleasant
Some animals protect themselves in **unpleasant** ways.

vile
A **vile** smell was coming from the kitchen.

→ loathsome; obnoxious

ANTONYM: pleasant

nervous ADJECTIVE

If you are **nervous**, you are worried about something.

anxious
He seemed **anxious**, so I asked him what was wrong.

jumpy
Our cat was **jumpy** every time we tried to look at the new kittens.

tense
My brother gets very **tense** before an exam.

worried
Mum was **worried** about cooking for so many people.

nice (1) ADJECTIVE

You say something is **nice** when you like it.

attractive
David's girlfriend is very **attractive**.

beautiful
Amy had a **beautiful** view of the sunset from her hotel room.

comfortable
The inside of Toad's caravan was surprisingly **comfortable**.

delicious
That big plate of cakes looks **delicious**.

enjoyable
The rabbits had a really **enjoyable** day eating the farmer's cabbages.

smart
Mr Magic loved his **smart** new cloak.

ANTONYM: horrible

nice (2) ADJECTIVE

If you are **nice** to people, you are friendly and kind.

friendly
I know my dog looks fierce, but he's really very **friendly**.

helpful
The people round here are **helpful**.

kind
It's **kind** of you to feed the tarantulas while I'm away.

ANTONYM: nasty

nice (3) ADJECTIVE
If you say the weather is **nice**, it is warm and pleasant.

fine
*Our cat will only go out when the weather's **fine**.*

sunny
*They went for a picnic on the first **sunny** day of the year.*

warm
*It was **warm** in the garden, so the children played outside.*

ANTONYM: bad

noise NOUN
A **noise** is a sound that someone or something makes.

clatter
*The **clatter** of cutlery told them that supper was ready.*

commotion
*During the **commotion**, Abhi managed to slip away.*

din
*The TV was on at full volume and Jackie had to yell above the **din**.*

racket
*Dad flung open the door and shouted, "Stop this **racket** at once!"*

row
*Jason's motorbike makes an awful **row**.*

noisy ADJECTIVE
Someone or something **noisy** makes loud or unpleasant sounds.

boisterous
*Dad complained the party was getting far too **boisterous**.*

deafening
*Suddenly there was a **deafening** clap of thunder.*

loud
*The boys' game was much too **loud**.*

piercing
*She was a nice girl, but they couldn't stand her **piercing** laugh.*
→ ear-splitting

ANTONYM: quiet

normal ADJECTIVE
Something that is **normal** is what you would expect.

average
*It's an **average** sort of house.*

everyday
*We eat pretty **everyday** foods, unless we're celebrating something.*

ordinary
*It was another **ordinary** day until the ghost appeared.*

usual
*The sisters were having their **usual** bedtime argument.*

Oo

odd ADJECTIVE

If you say something is **odd**, you mean it is strange or unusual.

funny
*Liam's teacher gave him a **funny** look.*

peculiar
*The sight of blood made her feel **peculiar**.*

strange
*They came to a huge door covered with **strange** pictures.*

weird
*A **weird** sound echoed through the castle and the children froze.*

→ bizarre

offend VERB

If you **offend** someone, you upset them by saying or doing something rude.

annoy
*Claire said she was sorry she had **annoyed** her grandmother.*

displease
*They found it was a mistake to **displease** the ogre.*

insult
*"Don't **insult** your brother," said Mum. "It's not funny."*

upset
*It will **upset** her if you criticize her hairstyle.*

often ADVERB

If something happens **often**, it happens many times.

again and again
*I've thought **again and again** of our lovely holiday in France.*

frequently
*They **frequently** found they'd eaten their lunch by eleven o'clock.*

regularly
*We try to visit the old lady **regularly** because she can't go out.*

repeatedly
*"I've told you **repeatedly**," said his mother, "to wipe your feet on the mat when you come in."*

time after time
Time after time they arrived late.

old (1) ADJECTIVE

Someone who is **old** has lived for a long time.

aged
*In the wood they met an **aged** man with a long white beard.*

elderly
*There were a lot of **elderly** people at the village meeting.*

ANTONYM: young

old (2) ADJECTIVE

Something that is **old** has existed for a long time.

ancient
*"There are a lot of **ancient** buildings in Rome," said Max.*

antique
*One room was full of **antique** clocks, all chiming at once.*

prehistoric
*The museum has a collection of **prehistoric** arrowheads.*

ANTONYM: modern

old (3) ADJECTIVE

Old can mean shabby or worn out.

shabby
There were only a couple of shabby armchairs to sit on.

tattered
The wizard's cloak was so tattered it looked as if mice had been at it.

worn out
Mum complained that her shoes were worn out.

ANTONYM: new

opening NOUN

An opening is a hole or space that things or people can go through.

break
The sun shone briefly through a break in the clouds.

chink
A chink between the curtains allowed a strip of light to escape.

crack
Smoke was rising through a crack between the floorboards.

hole
The boys peered into the garden through a hole in the fence.

slot
Dad's car keys fell down through a slot in the grating.

space
There was just a space where the door should have been.

opinion NOUN

An opinion is a belief or view.

belief
It's my belief that he is a very talented young artist.

view
You should make your views known to the head teacher.

order VERB

If someone orders you to do something, they tell you to do it.

command
The king commanded that his jester should be brought to him.

demand
"Give me all your money and jewels," demanded the highwayman.

instruct
Mr Blake instructed them to sit absolutely still while he took the register.

tell
The doctor told Nicky to stay in bed for a week.

ordinary ADJECTIVE

Something that is ordinary is not special in any way.

normal
It started out as just a normal day.

regular
His regular outfit was T-shirt and jeans.

routine
She took the dog on a routine walk round the park.

standard
They could only afford to buy the standard model.

usual
"Don't worry," said the doctor. "This is a usual complaint for someone your age."

→ common or garden; run-of-the-mill

ANTONYM: special

Pp

pain NOUN

A **pain** is an unpleasant feeling that you have in part of your body if you have been hurt or are ill.

ache
*She had a dull **ache** in her stomach.*

irritation
*The patchy, red rash was driving him mad with **irritation**.*

soreness
*Mum put a plaster on his grazed knee to help the **soreness**.*

trouble
*His bad tooth was giving him **trouble**.*

twinge
*Grandma complained of a **twinge** in her shoulder and back.*

→ agony; torture

pale ADJECTIVE

Something that is **pale** is without much colour.

colourless
*His favourite T-shirt was **colourless** from endless washing.*

faded
*There were **faded** stripes on the curtains where the sun had caught them.*

pasty
*He has a **pasty** complexion, as if he spends his life indoors.*

sallow
*Her face was **sallow** from a recent illness.*

wan
*She looked tired and **wan** after the journey.*

white
*Chloe turned **white** with shock.*

part NOUN

A **part** is a piece or section of something.

bit
*My favourite **bit** of the book is where he slew the dragon.*

fragment
*They recovered most of the broken bowl, but a **fragment** was still missing.*

piece
*There's one **piece** of the puzzle that remains to be solved.*

portion
*The sloping **portion** of the garden was hard to mow.*

section
*A **section** of the train had to be closed off.*

pattern (1) NOUN

A **pattern** is a diagram or shape used as a guide for making something.

design
*Dad drew up a **design** for the rabbit hutch.*

diagram
*A **diagram** showed how to build the model aircraft.*

plan
*We followed the **plan** exactly but the table still looked odd.*

stencil
*The pack included a **stencil** and paint for the lettering.*

template
*Hannah pinned the **template** of a skirt on the material and cut round it.*

pattern (2) NOUN

A **pattern** can be a design of repeated shapes.

arrangement
*Heather's new dress was blue with an **arrangement** of white flowers.*

design
*The wizard's cloak was covered in a **design** of stars and moons.*

pause NOUN

A **pause** is a short period when something stops.

break
*There was a **break** in the conversation when a stranger walked in.*

delay
*The clown announced a **delay** in his act while he hunted for his shoes.*

gap
*Sometimes TV programmes have **gaps** for advertisements.*

halt
*The games teacher signalled a **halt** in the race. Two children were running in the wrong direction.*

intermission
*The show started with advertisements, then there was an **intermission** before the animal film began.*

interruption
*Fire practice created an **interruption** in the lesson.*

interval
*Spencer went to get an ice cream in the **interval** between the acts.*

rest
*Mel demanded a **rest** before pressing on with the hike.*

peace NOUN

Peace is a feeling of quiet and calm.

calm
*Storm clouds were threatening to disturb the **calm** of the afternoon.*

quiet
*The **quiet** of the lane was a relief after the noisy motorway.*

silence
*Not even birdsong interrupted the perfect **silence** of the wood.*

stillness
*A screech from an owl shattered the **stillness** of the night.*

tranquillity
*The family moved to the country in search of **tranquillity**.*

persuade VERB

If someone **persuades** you to do something you did not want to do, you agree because they give you a good reason.

coax
*We **coaxed** Dad to take us to the zoo by saying it was educational.*

entice
*Raffy **enticed** the rabbit back into her hutch by putting a carrot in it.*

sway
*My sister is often **swayed** by clever advertisements on TV.*

tempt
*Henry **tempted** his brother to come by promising he'd see fox cubs.*

urge
*The head teacher **urged** us to consider after-school activities.*

a
b
c
d
e
f
g
h
i
j
k
l
m
n
o
Pp
q
r
s
t
u
v
w
x
y
z

pester

pester VERB

If you **pester** someone, you keep bothering them.

annoy
Can't you go and annoy someone else?

badger
Amy's little brother badgered her until she agreed to play with him.

bother
Don't bother Grandma now. She's trying to sleep.

nag
Sam kept nagging his dad to get him a new bike.

plague
They took a picnic to the river but were soon plagued by mosquitoes.

→ get on someone's nerves; drive someone up the wall

pick (1) VERB

To **pick** means to choose.

choose
We chose Kaitlin as our captain.

decide on
Timothy couldn't decide on a name for his ginger kitten.

select
The king selected the bravest knight to be his champion.

pick (2) VERB

When you **pick** flowers or fruit, you take them off the plant.

collect
The sisters went into the orchard to collect ripe plums.

cut
Nadia cut roses for the jug in the hall.

gathered
We went out to gather blackberries.

pluck
He tested each pear before plucking it from the tree.

picture (1) NOUN

A **picture** is a drawing, painting or photograph.

KINDS OF PICTURES:

cartoon	painting
collage	photograph
diagram	portrait
drawing	poster
map	print
mosaic	sketch
mural	

cartoon

diagram

map

picture (2) VERB

If you **picture** something in your mind, you can imagine it.

imagine
Katherine could imagine her friend's surprise when she opened the present.

see
He could see what was going to happen.

visualize
They tried to visualize what the new teacher would look like.

piece NOUN

A **piece** is a part of something.

bit
A **bit** of pie fell on the floor and the dog gobbled it up.

lump
Lumps of clay were lying on the table where the sculptor was working.

scrap
She was sewing together **scraps** of material to make a patchwork quilt.

shred
Our naughty puppy ripped the rug to **shreds**.

slab
The builder used large **slabs** of stone to make the patio.

slice
Nathan cut himself a **slice** of cake.

pile NOUN

A **pile** is a lot of things, such as books, which have been put one on top of the other.

heap
She nearly tripped over a **heap** of dirty washing left on the floor.

hoard
In the cave, they came upon a **hoard** of gold and silver.

mound
There was a curious **mound** of stones beside the path.

mountain
People had left a **mountain** of things for the jumble sale.

stack
A **stack** of books lay beside his chair, waiting to be read.

place (1) NOUN

A **place** is a building or area.

area
Uncle Peter wants to move to an **area** with lots of fields and trees.

district
This **district** doesn't have many shops.

house
It's an ordinary sort of **house**.

neighbourhood
Sasha and her family live in a very friendly **neighbourhood**.

spot
The barge was moored at a peaceful **spot** on the river.

place (2) VERB

If you **place** something somewhere, you put it there.

lay
Gwendolin **laid** the injured fairy in a cobweb hammock.

leave
"**Leave** the groceries by the back door, please," said Lesley.

plant
Her grandma **planted** hollyhocks next to the wall.

put
He **put** a deckchair in the shade of a tree.

set out
Mole and Ratty **set out** their picnic beside the river.

plain

plain (1)   ADJECTIVE

Something that is **plain** is simple with no decoration.

basic
*The furniture at the hostel was **basic**, but quite comfortable.*

modest
*Hitomi loved his hillside home even though it was very **modest**.*

ordinary
*It was an **ordinary** wooden table with no decoration.*

simple
*Dan only wanted a **simple** jam sandwich for tea.*

plain (2)   ADJECTIVE

Plain can mean clear and easy to see.

clear
*The meaning of her words was **clear**.*

obvious
*It was **obvious** that Tom was upset. His bottom lip was quivering.*

plan (1)   NOUN

If you have a **plan**, you have thought of a way of doing something.

idea
*Sam had an **idea** that was sure to work. His bike would be mended in no time.*

method
*The team needed a different **method** if it was going to succeed.*

scheme
*Emma thought of a clever **scheme** to raise money.*

system
*They all agreed the **system** was a failure.*

plan (2)   NOUN

A **plan** is a detailed drawing of something that is to be made.

design
*They loved the **design** for the robot.*

diagram
*"It's a spaceship **diagram**," said Ian.*

drawing
*The file contained a **drawing** that showed part of the new car's engine.*

layout
*Leonie studied the **layout** before she started building her model.*

plan (3)   VERB

If you **plan** what you are going to do, you decide how to do it.

aim
*Emilio **aimed** to be the new team captain.*

arrange
*"The spell works at dawn," said the witch. "You'd better **arrange** to be out."*

design
*The teacher **designed** tests to show each child's abilities.*

intend
*Captain Fantastic **intended** to land on the planet Jupiter.*

organize
*Mr Lewis **organized** a sack race for the parents.*

think about
*"It's no good rushing in," said Amanda. "We need to **think about** this."*

play (1) VERB

When you **play**, you spend time doing things you enjoy.

amuse yourself
*"Please **amuse yourselves** quietly while Grandpa has a rest," said Gran.*

have fun
*The cousins **had fun** in the paddling pool all afternoon.*

romp about
*Our garden is the sort of place where you can **romp about** safely.*

play (2) VERB

When one person or team **plays** another, they take part in a game and each side tries to win.

challenge
*He was good at tennis and was prepared to **challenge** anybody in his group.*

compete against
*Blues are **competing against** yellows in the next race.*

take on
*The girls' team is ready to **take on** the boys at football.*

play (3) NOUN

A **play** is a story that is acted on the stage, or on radio or television.

comedy
*There was a really funny **comedy** on television last night.*

drama
*Mum likes to hear radio **dramas**, especially if they have happy endings.*

performance
*Our class put on a terrific **performance** at the end of term.*

show
*On my birthday we're going to the theatre to see a **show**.*

tragedy
*It's a **tragedy** where everybody ends up getting killed.*

pleasant (1) ADJECTIVE

Something that is **pleasant** is enjoyable or attractive.

agreeable
*Mum painted the kitchen an **agreeable** shade of blue.*

charming
*It was a **charming** beach far away from the crowds.*

delightful
*Uncle Dave said they had a **delightful** view of the countryside from the hotel.*

enjoyable
*We spent an **enjoyable** afternoon fishing for shrimps in rock pools.*

refreshing
*After their walk, the girls cooled down in the **refreshing** breeze.*

satisfying
*They finished the day with a **satisfying** meal at the local restaurant.*

pleasant (2) ADJECTIVE

A person who is **pleasant** is friendly and likeable.

amiable
*I know you don't like her, but she always seems **amiable** to me.*

cheerful
*Everyone at the supermarket is **cheerful** and willing to help.*

friendly
*A **friendly** woman with a baby told them where to find the park.*

plot NOUN

A **plot** is a secret plan made by a group of people.

conspiracy
The pirate captain was sure there was a ***conspiracy*** *against him.*

plan
Guy Fawkes worked out a ***plan*** *to blow up the Houses of Parliament.*

scheme
The Sheriff of Nottingham thought up a ***scheme*** *to trap Robin Hood.*

poetry NOUN

Poetry is writing in which the lines have a rhythm and sometimes rhyme.

poem
They were asked to write ***poems*** *about something that interested them.*

rhyme
Jessie was good at thinking up funny ***rhymes*** *to entertain her friends.*

verse
The author handed out books of ***verse*** *for the children to look at.*

KINDS OF POETRY:

acrostic	haiku
ballad	jingle
blank verse	limerick
calligram	narrative poem
cinquain	nursery rhyme
concrete poem	ode
couplet	rap
elegy	shape poem
epic	sonnet
free verse	tanka

point NOUN

The **point** of something is the purpose or meaning it has.

aim
The main ***aim*** *of a thesaurus is to help you find words with similar meanings.*

goal
A leaflet explained that the ***goal*** *was to raise money for Children In Need.*

object
Nick's main ***object*** *in life was football.*

purpose
She couldn't see much ***purpose*** *in computer games.*

poke VERB

If you **poke** someone, you quickly push them with your finger or a sharp object.

jab
"Don't speak to me like that!" he shouted, ***jabbing*** *her shoulder.*

nudge
Ranjit giggled and ***nudged*** *his friend in the ribs with an elbow.*

prod
Esther ***prodded*** *the bulge in her little brother's pocket. "What have you got in there?" she asked.*

polite ADJECTIVE

Someone who is **polite** has good manners and thinks about other people's feelings.

civil
You don't have to like her, but you can at least be ***civil***.

courteous
He was a ***courteous*** *man who always raised his hat to a woman.*

respectful
She was brought up to be ***respectful*** *to older people.*

well-mannered
"It's nice to see such a ***well-mannered*** *little boy," she said.*

Pp

poor ADJECTIVE
Someone who is **poor** has very little money and few possessions.

broke INFORMAL
*Alex says he's too **broke** to go out with us.*

deprived
*This is a very **deprived** area.*

hard up INFORMAL
*If you're so **hard up**, how can you afford those trainers?*

pour VERB
To **pour** means to flow quickly and in large amounts.

gush
*Blood **gushed** from the dragon's wounds.*

run
*The heavy rain **ran** down the gutters.*

spill
*Water **spilled** everywhere as Jack dropped his bucket.*

stream
*Tears **streamed** down Rachel's face.*

→ bucket down; come down in torrents; rain cats and dogs

power NOUN
The **power** of something, such as the wind or the sea, is its strength.

force
*The **force** of the wind blew a branch across the road.*

strength
*Trees near our cottage could not stand against the **strength** of the storm.*

private ADJECTIVE
If something is **private**, only a few people know about it.

confidential
*Don't tell anyone else. It's **confidential**.*

quiet
*Clare had her own **quiet** place at the end of the garden.*

secluded
*The beach was **secluded**, so they could swim in peace.*

secret
*Sean took them in through a **secret** door.*

solitary
*The wizard lived in a **solitary** cottage, tucked away in the wood.*

problem (1) NOUN
A **problem** is something that is difficult.

complication
*"There's a **complication**, I'm afraid," he said. "There aren't any boats to take you to your holiday island."*

difficulty
*"We can soon sort out that little **difficulty**," said Sophie.*

trouble
*"If you have any **trouble** finding your size, just ask," said the shop assistant.*

→ can of worms; hard nut to crack

problem (2) NOUN
A **problem** can also be something like a puzzle that you have to work out.

brain-teaser
*Kate spent many happy hours solving all sorts of **brain-teasers**.*

puzzle
*Dad's brilliant at crossword **puzzles**.*

question
*Nobody could do the last **question**.*

riddle
*They had to think very hard about the **riddle** before they knew what to do.*

121

promise

promise VERB

If you **promise** to do something, you mean you really will do it.

assure
Graham **assured** us he'd have the car ready by Friday.

give your word
Jessica **gave her word** she'd be home by five o'clock.

guarantee
The shop assistant **guaranteed** the colours wouldn't run.

vow
Caroline **vowed** she wouldn't tell anyone the secret.

→ cross your heart; swear

proper ADJECTIVE

The **proper** thing is the one that is correct or most suitable.

apt
It was hard to find an **apt** description for the wizard's strange behaviour.

correct
You must fill the space in each sentence with the **correct** word.

fitting
The applause was a **fitting** end to such a wonderful play.

right
I'd like to know the **right** name for my new plant.

suitable
We don't have a **suitable** tool to deal with that job.

protect VERB

To **protect** someone or something is to prevent them from being harmed.

defend
He's always ready to **defend** his little brother in the playground.

guard
Our dog **guards** the house by barking at anyone it doesn't know.

look after
"You must **look after** your hamster when the cat's around," said Mum, "or he'll get eaten."

shelter
A shed in the field **shelters** the donkey in bad weather.

shield
Alice's umbrella **shielded** her from the pouring rain.

proud ADJECTIVE

If you feel **proud**, you feel glad about something you have done, or about something that belongs to you.

glad
Our team was **glad** to win the cup after all that hard work.

gratified
The actors were **gratified** when the audience rose to its feet and cheered.

honoured
Uncle Jim says he is **honoured** to be chosen as a judge at the pet show.

pleased
Rosie's parents were so **pleased** when she came top of the class.

pull VERB

When you **pull** something, you hold it firmly and move it towards you.

drag
*Sebastian **dragged** out his train set from the cupboard.*

draw
*"**Draw** that chair nearer to the fire and keep warm," said Gran.*

haul
*Daisy **hauled** a jumper from her bag.*

heave
*Between them they managed to **heave** the sack into the garage.*

tow
*The car broke down and we had to get a truck to **tow** us home.*

tug
*Simon **tugged** as hard as he could, but his friend was stuck.*

ANTONYM: push

pure ADJECTIVE

Something that is **pure** is not mixed with anything else.

clean
*It is much healthier and more pleasant to breathe **clean** air.*

clear
*They drank **clear** water that bubbled up from the spring.*

natural
*Ruth liked the feel of **natural** silk against her skin.*

real
*Mum always buys **real** fruit juices for us to drink at break.*

unmixed
*When she saw her old friend she felt **unmixed** joy.*

unpolluted
*Far from the motorway, the atmosphere was **unpolluted**.*

push VERB

When you **push** something, you press it hard.

force
*There was a huge crowd and the children had to **force** their way to the front.*

poke
*Bertha **poked** a stick in the sand.*

press
***Press** the doorbell so Charlie knows we have arrived.*

thrust
*Sir Jasper **thrust** his sword into the dragon's belly.*

ANTONYM: pull

put VERB

When you **put** something somewhere, you move it there.

arrange
*Mum **arranged** the flowers in a vase.*

dump
*Stephen came in and **dumped** his bag in the hall.*

lay
*She **laid** the baby in his cot and sang a quiet lullaby.*

leave
*They **left** newspapers and glass bottles in the blue box to be recycled.*

pile
*Matilda **piled** the library books beside her bedroom chair.*

place
*Trevor **placed** the insect on his hand for the others to see.*

set out
*They **set out** the chess pieces on the board.*

quality

a
b
c
d
e
f
g
h
i
j
k
l
m
n
o
p
Qq
r
s
t
u
v
w
x
y
z

quality NOUN

The **quality** of something is how good or bad it is, compared with other things of the same kind.

excellence
*It was a chance to show the **excellence** of their work.*

grade
*King Henry's tailor always used cloth of the finest **grade**.*

standard
*"I expect your writing to be of a high **standard**," said the teacher.*

value
*Things from that greengrocer are always good **value**.*

quarrel NOUN

A **quarrel** is an angry argument.

argument
*I've just had an **argument** with my friend and she won.*

disagreement
*There was a **disagreement** about the seating in class.*

fight
*My brothers had a **fight** over the train set.*

row
*The washing-up often leads to a **row** in our house.*

squabble
*The girls had a silly **squabble** then quickly made friends again.*

question VERB

If you **question** someone or something, you try to find something out.

ask
*The police officer **asked** him about his movements that night.*

interrogate
*Spencer **interrogated** everyone who might have seen his lost guinea pig.*

probe into
*They decided to **probe into** the reasons for her behaviour.*

quiz
*Meredith **quizzed** her about her job as a nanny.*

quick (1) ADJECTIVE

Someone or something that is **quick** moves very fast.

brisk
*The family went for a **brisk** walk through the park.*

fast
*Albert was a surprisingly **fast** elephant.*

hurried
*I could tell by her **hurried** greeting that she didn't have time to chat.*

rapid
*With a **rapid** movement, the conjuror made the watch vanish.*

speedy
*The mouse found his cage door open and made a **speedy** exit.*

→ like lightning; in a flash

ANTONYM: **slow**

quick (2) ADJECTIVE

Something that is **quick** lasts only a short time.

brief
*We had a **brief** talk in the playground.*

hurried
*They had a **hurried** meal before going to the cinema.*

swift
*The robot read a whole page with a **swift** movement of its eye.*

ANTONYM: long

quick (3) ADJECTIVE

Quick can mean happening without any delay.

prompt
*"No, there's nobody here," came the **prompt** reply.*

sudden
*The cat made a **sudden** jump and caught a mouse by its tail.*

quiet (1) ADJECTIVE

Someone or something that is **quiet** makes little noise or no noise at all.

low
*"I think he's coming now," said Rupert in a **low** voice.*

shy
*Vanessa was a **shy** little girl.*

silent
*The teacher glared at them. "You must be **silent** for at least two minutes."*

soft
*There was a **soft** sound of purring coming from the bed.*

timid
*"Don't be so **timid**," said Zina. "Speak up for yourself."*

➔ quiet as a mouse

ANTONYM: noisy

quiet (2) ADJECTIVE

Quiet means peaceful.

calm
*Things soon became **calm** again after the boys' squabble.*

hushed
*The whole room was **hushed** as the head teacher began to speak.*

peaceful
*Mum had a lovely **peaceful** time when the children went back to school.*

quite (1) ADVERB

Quite can mean rather.

fairly
*She could run **fairly** fast.*

rather
*The sea was **rather** choppy.*

quite (2) ADVERB

Quite can mean completely.

absolutely
*We were **absolutely** worn out when we arrived home.*

completely
*Are you **completely** finished now?*

fully
*The dragon said he **fully** understood the problem he'd caused.*

a b c d e f g h i j k l m n o p **Qq** r s t u v w x y z

Rr

ready ADJECTIVE

If someone or something is **ready**, they are properly prepared for something.

organized
"Everything was organized for the picnic when it began to pour with rain," explained Auntie Anne.

prepared
Hamish wasn't sure he was prepared to say his lines.

ripe
The fruit had to be ripe before they would eat it.

set
Ten minutes later, they were all set to go to the park.

real (1) ADJECTIVE

Something that is **real** is true. It is not imaginary.

actual
The actual story of what happened was quite different.

genuine
Her tales of the mysterious figure in the wood are genuine.

true
They watched a film that was based on a true adventure.

ANTONYM: imaginary

real (2) ADJECTIVE

You can say **real** when you mean the thing itself and not a copy.

authentic
My great-grandpa has an authentic air-force jacket.

genuine
The man told them the painting was a genuine Rembrandt.

true
She tried to hide her true feelings about the boy.

ANTONYM: fake

reptile NOUN

A **reptile** is a cold-blooded animal with a scaly skin. Female reptiles lay eggs.

SOME REPTILES:

alligator	lizard
crocodile	snake
dinosaur (extinct)	tortoise
gecko	turtle

alligator

lizard

snake

turtle

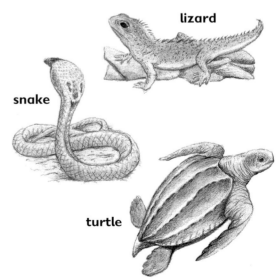

rest (1) VERB

When you **rest**, you sit or lie down and keep still for a while.

put your feet up
Grandma **puts her feet up** after lunch.

relax
At the weekend Alex liked to **relax** and read his book.

sit down
Sabrina said if she didn't **sit down** she'd fall down.

take it easy
"Well done," said the teacher. "Now you can **take it easy** for a while."

rest (2) NOUN

A **rest** is a period of time when you do not work.

break
Take a **break** now, and come back here in ten minutes.

holiday
Dad says he could do with a long **holiday**.

pause
After a short **pause** she continued reading the story.

rest (3) NOUN

The **rest** is all the things in a group that are left.

leftovers
Some of the food vanished at the party. We put the **leftovers** in the fridge.

others
Emma finished her work and went home. The **others** had to stay.

remainder
Put a deposit on the bike now, and pay the **remainder** when you collect it.

right (1) ADJECTIVE

If something is **right**, it is correct.

accurate
Your measurements must be **accurate**, or it won't fit.

correct
If the information is **correct**, we'll take off at 11 o'clock.

exact
It's no good guessing. I need to know the **exact** answer.

spot-on INFORMAL
Harriet's maths work was always **spot-on**.

true
It was an interesting story, but William wasn't sure it was **true**.

ANTONYM: wrong

right (2) ADJECTIVE

Right also means the most suitable.

appropriate
He asked what would be the **appropriate** thing to do.

ideal
They all thought Ashley would be the **ideal** team leader.

proper
Robin spent ages finding the **proper** words to describe his hero.

suitable
The tiny flat wasn't **suitable** as a home for a large dog.

rise

rise (1) VERB

If something **rises**, it moves upwards.

ascend
*The lift **ascended** with great speed.*

climb
*Next year, the number of children in the school will **climb** rapidly.*

get to your feet
*They all **got to their feet** and cheered.*

get up
*"What time do you **get up** in the morning?" asked Sophia.*

soar
*We watched the kite **soar** into the sky.*

stand up
*Edward had to **stand up** when his name was called.*

take off
*The plane **took off** and disappeared above the clouds.*

rise (2) VERB

To **rise** can mean to increase.

go up
*My pocket money will **go up** next week, I hope.*

grow
*TV chiefs expected viewing numbers to **grow** quickly.*

improve
*Pass rates in the test have **improved** again this year.*

increase
*At the moment, prices are still **increasing**.*

ANTONYM: fall

rough (1) ADJECTIVE

If something is **rough**, the surface is uneven and not smooth.

bumpy
*Our car jerked all over the place on the **bumpy** road.*

craggy
*They gazed in dismay at the **craggy** mountainside above them.*

rocky
*A lighthouse can signal warnings of a **rocky** coastline.*

uneven
*The track was **uneven** and she stumbled several times.*

ANTONYM: smooth

rough (2) ADJECTIVE

Rough can mean difficult or unpleasant.

difficult
*Miss Honey had quite a **difficult** life with her aunt.*

hard
*Charles Dickens wrote about **hard** times in Victorian England.*

tough
*A fisherman's job can be very **tough**.*

uncomfortable
*We had an **uncomfortable** ride in a donkey cart.*

unpleasant
*Cinderella had to do all the **unpleasant** work in the house.*

ANTONYM: easy

a b c d e f g h i j k l m n o p q Rr s t u v w x y z

rough (3)   ADJECTIVE

A **rough** estimate is not meant to be exact.

approximate
*Work out the **approximate** size of the school playground.*

estimated
*The **estimated** cost of the building sounded reasonable.*

sketchy
*Kylie had only a **sketchy** idea of how the thing worked.*

vague
*Charles could give only a **vague** description of the man.*

ANTONYM: exact

ruin   VERB

To **ruin** something means to spoil it completely.

demolish
*They are **demolishing** a big house to make way for flats.*

destroy
*Trees fell in a violent storm and **destroyed** a beautiful garden.*

smash
*A car swerved off the road and **smashed** the fence.*

wreck
*Some large animals trampled on our tent and **wrecked** it.*

run (1)   VERB

When you **run**, you move quickly, leaving the ground during each stride.

bolt
*The horse **bolted**, dragging the cart with it.*

dash
*"Is that the right time?" asked Rosemary. "I must **dash**."*

gallop
*The pony **galloped** across the common.*

hurry
*"There's no need to **hurry**," said Danny.*

race
*They had to **race** to the sweetshop before it closed.*

scamper
*Mice **scampered** across the floor of the old water mill.*

run (2)   VERB

Someone who **runs** something, like a school or country, is in charge of it.

be in charge of
*The head teacher **is in charge of** our school. She's called Ms Johns.*

lead
*We need another person to **lead** our swimming group.*

look after
*Jamal was asked to **look after** the stationery cupboard.*

manage
*Clare's dad **manages** the supermarket in our town.*

sad

Ss

sad (1) ADJECTIVE

If you are **sad**, you are unhappy because something has happened that you do not like.

dejected
They all felt **dejected** when the birthday party was cancelled.

gloomy
Eeyore was a very **gloomy** animal.

miserable
I tried to cheer up my big sister when she felt **miserable**.

tearful
Ranjit was **tearful** when his budgie died.

unhappy
I had never seen James look so **unhappy**.

ANTONYM: happy

sad (2) ADJECTIVE

Things that are **sad** make you feel unhappy.

depressing
Dad didn't like the film. He said it was too **depressing**.

disappointing
It was **disappointing** when the storybook prince and princess didn't get married.

dismal
It was an exciting game but the final score was **dismal**.

dreadful
There was news of a **dreadful** loss of life in the earthquake.

tragic
Harry Potter learned of the **tragic** death of his parents.

safe (1) ADJECTIVE

If you are **safe**, you are not in any danger.

out of harm's way
"Luckily, everyone was **out of harm's way** when the floods came," explained the town spokesperson.

protected
Wildlife is **protected** in nature reserves across the country.

secure
Charlie loved being tucked up in bed. It made him feel **secure**.

undamaged
Emily picked up the crying baby. "It's okay, you're **undamaged**," she said.

unhurt
Mehmet crawled out from the wreckage, stood up, and was surprised to find he was **unhurt**.

→ safe and sound; safe as houses

safe (2) ADJECTIVE

If something is **safe**, it does not cause harm or danger.

harmless
They thought the snake was poisonous, but it was **harmless**.

pure
A scientist tested the water to make sure it was **pure**.

unpolluted
Anna walked deep into the woods where the air was **unpolluted**.

ANTONYM: dangerous

satisfactory ADJECTIVE

Something that is **satisfactory** is good enough for its purpose.

acceptable
*The king seemed to find the jester's silly jokes **acceptable**.*

adequate
*"Portions of food are rather small in our canteen," said Gregory, "but they're just about **adequate**."*

all right
*"I suppose the holiday was **all right**," Melek admitted.*

good enough
*"Your excuse is not **good enough**," said the teacher. "I do not want you to be late again."*

passable
*Silvester produced a **passable** portrait of his friend.*

tolerable
*She spent a **tolerable** afternoon watching the cricket.*

satisfy VERB

To **satisfy** someone means to give them what they want.

content
*The cat **contented** herself with a patch of sun to lie in.*

fill
*His new friend **filled** his need for company of his own age.*

please
*You can always **please** Mum with chocolates on her birthday.*

save (1) VERB

If you **save** someone or something, you help them escape from harm or danger.

free
*They managed to **free** a bird that was caught in some netting.*

liberate
*Kylie was tangled in brambles but her mum soon **liberated** her.*

release
*Theodore **released** his hamster from the cat's jaws.*

rescue
*A dog **rescued** its owners by barking when the fire started.*

salvage
*The shipwrecked sailor managed to **salvage** a number of tools.*

save (2) VERB

If you **save** money, you gradually collect it by not spending it all.

hoard
*The king **hoarded** his wealth while the courtiers went around in rags.*

keep
*Auntie Mavis likes to **keep** a bit of cash for special treats.*

put aside
*I **put aside** some of my pocket money every week.*

reserve
*Mrs Jones always **reserves** some of her pension in case she needs it later.*

say

say VERB
When you **say** something, you speak words.

announce
The giraffe **announced** the winner of the knobbly knees contest.

answer
Esther called, "Who's there?" "It's only me," **answered** Joe.

ask
"Can you come to my party?" **asked** Ben. "We're having a cake."

claim
Abdul **claimed** there was a monster under his bed.

complain
"I haven't any friends left," **complained** the dragon.

confess
"I'm not really brave," **confessed** the stuntman. "I'm scared of beetles."

emphasize
"You must be home by midnight," **emphasized** Cinderella's fairy godmother.

exclaim
"Oh no!" she **exclaimed**. "My hair has turned green!"

hint
Grandma **hinted** she'd like a skateboard for her birthday.

hiss
"S-stay here where I can s-see you," **hissed** the snake.

insist
The king **insisted** he was going to sing a song he'd composed.

laugh
"You can't catch me," **laughed** Sam, and swung up into a tree.

murmur
"I'm rather timid," **murmured** the fairy.

promise
Promise you won't bring that rat into school again.

pronounce
She **pronounced** her name clearly.

read out
The princess **read out** her piece and everyone clapped.

recite
The children fell about laughing as Tom **recited** his limericks.

remark
"I may be slow," **remarked** the tortoise, "but at least I get there."

repeat
Sunita had to **repeat** her question twice.

reply
"What are you supposed to be?" asked the judge. "An astronaut," **replied** Tim.

snap
"Go away," he **snapped**. "I'm busy."

stammer
"H-h-help!" **stammered** the boy. "It's a spaceship!"

scarce ADJECTIVE

Something that is **scarce** is not often found.

few and far between
*Buses are **few and far between** in this part of the world.*

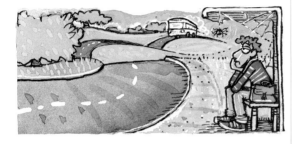

in short supply
*In some countries, food and medicines are **in short supply**.*

rare
*Birds of prey are becoming quite **rare** in some areas.*

thin on the ground
*Volunteers for this cleaning project are a bit **thin on the ground**.*

uncommon
*Only a few years ago computers were **uncommon**, but now lots of people have them at home.*

unusual
*"That type of stamp is **unusual**," said the collector. "I've only seen one before."*

scare VERB

Someone or something that **scares** you makes you feel frightened.

alarm
*The expression on the wizard's face **alarmed** them.*

frighten
*The wild wood **frightened** mole.*

startle
*Suddenly, a barn owl screeched and **startled** him.*

terrify
*The ogre **terrified** everybody.*

scatter VERB

If you **scatter** things, you throw or drop a lot of them all over an area.

fling
*The children **flung** the papers in the air in excitement.*

litter
*Clothes were **littered** all over Lewis's bedroom floor.*

sow
*As fast as Grandpa **sowed** his seeds, the birds gobbled them up.*

spread
*"**Spread** the corn evenly," she said, "so that all the chickens get some."*

sprinkle
*Mum carefully **sprinkled** drops of water on the seedlings.*

scrape (1) VERB

If you **scrape** something, you rub a rough or sharp object over it.

scratch
*Daniel accidentally **scratched** the table with his model car.*

scuff
*Libby tripped and **scuffed** her new shoes on the path.*

scrape (2) VERB

If something **scrapes** against something else, it makes a harsh noise.

grate
*The hinges **grated** as the old iron gate swung open.*

grind
*Farmer Brown's cartwheels **ground** against the gravel.*

rasp
*Stefan's hand **rasped** across the stubble on his chin.*

squeak
*A knife **squeaked** on the plate and set his teeth on edge.*

scream

scream VERB

If you **scream**, you shout or cry in a loud high-pitched voice.

howl

Bernard **howled** with pain when the pony stood on his foot.

screech

"How dare you ruin my spell!" **screeched** the witch.

shriek

We **shrieked** with laughter at his jokes.

squeal

The piglet **squealed** when they picked it up.

yell

"Help!" he **yelled**. "I've fallen in a ditch."

search VERB

If you **search** for something, you try to find it.

cast around

Philip **cast around** for an excuse not to go on the trip.

comb

They **combed** the field, looking for her missing purse.

hunt

Ben's football boots couldn't be found, though he **hunted** high and low.

look

Jessie **looked** everywhere, but there was no sign of her book.

scour

The dog **scoured** the whole garden until he found his bone.

secret ADJECTIVE

Something **secret** is known about by only a small number of people.

hidden

Joe had a **hidden** den in the bushes at the bottom of the garden.

out-of-the-way

They knew an **out-of-the-way** place where they could hold their meetings.

private

Her diary was **private** and nobody was allowed to read it.

secluded

The cottage had its own **secluded** beach.

→ cloak and dagger

see (1) VERB

If you **see** something, you are looking at it or you notice it.

glimpse

Out of the corner of his eye, Gary **glimpsed** a tiny creature.

notice

"Have you **noticed** my new trousers?" Mandy demanded.

observe

Astronomers **observed** strange marks on the planet's surface.

spot

The boys **spotted** Lauren creeping along behind the bushes.

watch

The wolf **watched** Little Red Riding Hood walk through the forest.

see (2) VERB

To **see** something also means to understand it.

follow
*They couldn't quite **follow** what the teacher was trying to say.*

get
*"I don't **get** the joke," said Henry.*

grasp
*She quickly **grasped** what was going on.*

realize
*Alice **realized** that something very curious was happening.*

understand
*Logan was the first to **understand** how the plan would work.*

seize VERB

If you **seize** something, you grab it firmly.

clutch
*The train stopped suddenly. Angela almost fell and had to **clutch** a seat.*

grab
*Rashid **grabbed** his bag and sprinted for the bus.*

grasp
*The old lady **grasped** Katherine's arm and asked for help.*

snatch
*A robber tried to **snatch** her purse, but she held on tightly.*

sensible ADJECTIVE

People who are **sensible** know what is the right thing to do.

down-to-earth
*My Auntie Hyacinth must be the most **down-to-earth** person I know.*

practical
*When you get in a muddle, you need someone **practical** to help you out.*

reasonable
*He's always so **reasonable** you can't argue with him.*

sound
*Most of her ideas are pretty **sound**.*

wise
*It might be **wise** to get home before it begins to rain.*

ANTONYM: foolish

sensitive (1) ADJECTIVE

If you are **sensitive**, you are easily upset about something.

easily upset
*She is **easily upset** when people won't eat her cooking.*

thin-skinned
*Kim is very **thin-skinned**, and cries easily.*

touchy
*My dad's rather **touchy** about the dent in his car.*

sensitive (2) ADJECTIVE

If something is **sensitive**, it is easily affected.

delicate
*The fairy's wings were far too **delicate** to touch.*

fine
*The baby has to stay out of the sun because of her **fine** skin.*

responsive
*Some flowers are **responsive** to daylight. They close at night.*

a
b
c
d
e
f
g
h
i
j
k
l
m
n
o
p
q
r
Ss
t
u
v
w
x
y
z

separate

separate ADJECTIVE

If two things are **separate**, they are not connected.

detached
My friend lives in a house that's **detached** from the one next door.

divided
A low fence keeps the play area **divided** from the rest of the garden.

isolated
The children with measles were kept **isolated** from the others.

serious (1) ADJECTIVE

Things that are **serious** are very bad and worrying.

bad
Flooding was particularly **bad** in low-lying areas.

dreadful
The storm caused **dreadful** problems for ships at sea.

severe
In some countries there is a **severe** shortage of food.

terrible
There was a **terrible** accident on the motorway near here.

worrying
The colonel reported a **worrying** lack of supplies at the camp.

serious (2) ADJECTIVE

Serious can mean important and needing careful thought.

difficult
We need to think carefully about this. It could be **difficult**.

important
The head teacher had an **important** announcement to make.

no laughing matter
They soon found that missing school was **no laughing matter**.

serious (3) ADJECTIVE

Someone who is **serious** is sincere about something.

genuine
The man made Dad a **genuine** offer for the car.

in earnest
The coach was **in earnest** about our need to practise.

sincere
Daisy had a **sincere** wish to help old people when she grew up.

serious (4) ADJECTIVE

People who are **serious** are often quiet and do not laugh very much.

grave
The wizard looked **grave**. "I can't help," he admitted.

solemn
Tommy was a **solemn** little boy, but we made him laugh.

thoughtful
She had a **thoughtful** look on her face.

settle VERB

If you **settle** something, you decide or arrange it.

agree
*"We need to **agree** a date for the first rehearsal," said Rachel.*

decide
*Have you **decided** where the party's going to be?*

resolve
*The captain is still trying to **resolve** the problem of the stowaway.*

shake (1) VERB

If something or someone **shakes**, they move from side to side or up and down.

quake
*The dragon stood **quaking** as the knight drew his sword.*

shiver
*Simon **shivered** with cold and wished he'd brought his jacket.*

shudder
*Maria **shuddered** with fear when she saw the snake.*

tremble
*We felt the ground **tremble** as the giant came near.*

vibrate
*When our old car was running, everything on it used to **vibrate**.*

wobble
*"Don't let the jelly **wobble** too much," warned Mum.*

shake (2) VERB

If you **shake** something, it moves from side to side or up and down.

agitate
***Agitate** the liquid until it becomes cloudy.*

brandish
*The knight galloped towards his foe, **brandishing** a sword over his head.*

flourish
*Mehmet **flourished** his letter. "I've won!" he shouted.*

waggle
*She **waggled** her fingers at the baby to make him laugh.*

wave
*Passengers **wave** handkerchiefs when their ship sails away.*

shake (3) VERB

If something **shakes** you, it shocks and upsets you.

distress
*The bad news was bound to **distress** her.*

disturb
*The noise of the fireworks **disturbed** the animals.*

rattle
*Abel was staring into space. Something had obviously **rattled** him.*

shock
*The accident **shocked** Grandpa.*

unnerve
*The size of the rock he was expected to climb **unnerved** Calum.*

upset
*The phone call **upset** Chloe.*

a b c d e f g h i j k l m n o p q r **Ss** t u v w x y z

shape

a
b
c
d
e
f
g
h
i
j
k
l
m
n
o
p
q
r
Ss
t
u
v
w
x
y
z

shape (1) NOUN

The **shape** of something is the form of its outline.

figure
The **figure** of a man emerged from the morning mist.

form
Suddenly the witch took on the **form** of a toad.

outline
In the poor light they could see only the **outline** of an animal.

shape (2) NOUN

A **shape** is something that has its outside edges joining in a particular way. Shapes can be flat, like a circle or triangle, or solid, like a cube or sphere.

FLAT SHAPES:

circle	oblong	rectangle
diamond	octagon	semicircle
heptagon	oval	square
hexagon	pentagon	star
kite	quadrilateral	triangle

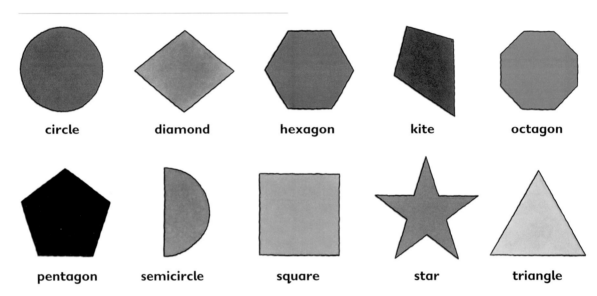

circle   diamond   hexagon   kite   octagon

pentagon   semicircle   square   star   triangle

SOLID SHAPES:

cone	hemisphere
cube	pyramid
cuboid	sphere
cylinder	

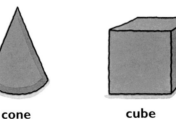

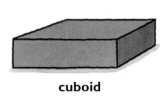

cone   cube   cuboid

cylinder   hemisphere   pyramids   sphere

share VERB

If you **share** something among a group of people, you divide it so that everyone gets some.

divide
They divided the chocolate cake into eight equal pieces.

split
Our school decided to split the money between two charities.

sharp (1) ADJECTIVE

A **sharp** object has a fine edge or point that is good for cutting or piercing things.

jagged
Roderick cut himself on a jagged piece of glass.

keen
Be careful with that knife. It has a very keen blade.

pointed
Marianne used a pointed stick to write a message in the sand.

ANTONYM: blunt

sharp (2) ADJECTIVE

A **sharp** person is quick to notice or understand things.

bright
Only bright people can go on this television quiz show.

clever
A clever vet instantly knew what was wrong with our hamster.

observant
The baby is really observant. She noticed my earrings.

quick
Duncan is quick. You only have to tell him something once.

quick-witted
Samuel was quick-witted enough to foil the burglar.

shelter NOUN

A **shelter** is a small building or covered place where people or animals can be safe from bad weather or danger.

cover
When it started to pour, they ran for cover.

protection
The stable gave the horse protection from bad weather.

refuge
They took refuge from the storm in an old barn.

safety
Just in time, the rabbit dived for the safety of its burrow.

screen
A high wall provided a screen for tender young plants.

shine VERB

If something **shines**, it gives out a bright light.

flash
A lantern flashed in the window of the broken-down old house.

flicker
Rosita's candle flickered as she climbed the stairs.

glimmer
Lanterns glimmered in the garden.

glow
The magic stone glowed in the half-light of the cave.

twinkle
It was a fine night, and stars twinkled in the sky.

a
b
c
d
e
f
g
h
i
j
k
l
m
n
o
p
q
r
Ss
t
u
v
w
x
y
z

short

short (1) ADJECTIVE

Someone or something **short** is small in height.

little
On the corner of the house was a *little* tower.

low
There was a **low** fence around the children's play area.

small
Becky was **small** for her age, so she played younger parts in the drama group.

tiny
The elf was so **tiny** he could comfortably sit on a mushroom.

ANTONYM: tall

short (2) ADJECTIVE

A **short** period of time does not last very long.

brief
The head teacher gave a **brief** talk before lessons began.

fleeting
"We've only got time for a **fleeting** visit," said Whitney.

momentary
There was a **momentary** pause before he spoke again.

quick
"We could take a **quick** break now, if you're tired," he said.

shout VERB

If you **shout** something, you say it very loudly.

bellow
"What are you doing in my field?" **bellowed** the farmer.

call
Michelle twisted her ankle and had to **call** for help.

cry
"Let me do it!" she **cried**.

roar
"I know you!" he **roared**. "You're the ones who broke my window."

scream
They **screamed** with terror when they saw the ghost.

yell
"You don't have to **yell** like that," said Mum. "I can hear you perfectly well."

show (1) VERB

If you **show** someone how to do something, you do it yourself so that they can watch you.

demonstrate
The teacher **demonstrated** how to use a camera.

explain
Grandma asked me to **explain** how the computer worked.

teach
Christopher **taught** his little sister how to draw horses.

a
b
c
d
e
f
g
h
i
j
k
l
m
n
o
p
q
r
Ss
t
u
v
w
x
y
z

show (2) VERB

If you **show** someone something, you let them see it.

display
*Sean **displayed** his project with the others.*

exhibit
*At the end of term the children **exhibited** their paintings.*

reveal
*The captured spy was unwilling to **reveal** his true identity.*

show (3) NOUN

A **show** is something that you watch, sometimes at the theatre or on television.

display
*There was a huge **display** of fireworks on bonfire night.*

exhibition
*The local art club is having an **exhibition** next week.*

performance
*Emma had never been on television before and was nervous about the **performance**.*

show (4) VERB

If you **show** that something is true, you prove it.

confirm
*"Can you **confirm** you were at home last night?" asked the police officer.*

demonstrate
*Julian **demonstrated** his honesty by handing in the money he had found.*

prove
*Rosie **proved** she could look after a pet.*

shrill ADJECTIVE

A **shrill** sound is loud and high-pitched, like a whistle.

high-pitched
*The sound was so **high-pitched** he had to clap his hands over his ears.*

piercing
*Johnny let out a **piercing** cry when the animal bit him.*

screeching
*The children knew that there was an owl outside. It kept them awake with its **screeching** call.*

sharp
*The signal was to be a **sharp** blast on the captain's whistle.*

→ ear-piercing; ear-splitting

shut VERB

If you **shut** something such as a door, you move it so that it fills a gap.

close
*They were asked to **close** gates after them, to stop animals straying.*

fasten
*The queen checked her jewels and **fastened** the box.*

lock
*We **locked** the door of the hutch to keep the rabbit safe.*

slam
*We could tell Alexandra was cross again. There was a loud bang as she **slammed** the kitchen door.*

ANTONYM: open

shy ADJECTIVE

A **shy** person or animal is nervous with people they do not know well.

cautious
*Our cat is **cautious** with strangers.*

modest
*She's very **modest** and doesn't like to talk about her achievements.*

nervous
*I feel a bit **nervous** when I have to read things out in class.*

timid
*Her brother looks tough, but he's as **timid** as a mouse.*

wary
*Andrew's new dog is **wary** of anyone it doesn't know.*

ANTONYM: bold

silent ADJECTIVE

If someone or something is **silent**, they do not say anything or make any noise.

dumb
*They were all **dumb** with amazement at the sight of the castle.*

quiet
*It was unusually **quiet** in the wood now everything was covered in snow.*

soundless
*Her footsteps were **soundless** as she moved swiftly across the floor.*

wordless
*Peter watched the dancers' performance in **wordless** admiration.*

silly ADJECTIVE

If someone says you are **silly**, they mean you are behaving in a foolish or childish way.

daft
*I don't know where you get your **daft** ideas.*

foolish
*"That was a **foolish** thing to do," said the class teacher.*

idiotic
*He wanted us to play some **idiotic** game.*

ridiculous
*Some people came on the trek wearing **ridiculous** shoes.*

stupid
*I was **stupid** enough to listen to him.*

skip VERB

When you **skip**, you step forward and hop, first with one foot and then the other.

bounce
*She jumped up in delight and **bounced** over to greet him.*

caper
*The jester made jokes and **capered** before the king.*

dance
*To their amazement, a fairy **danced** lightly across the grass in front of them.*

hop
*She **hopped** over the rope as they spun it faster and faster.*

leap
*He tried to catch her, but she **leaped** away, laughing wildly.*

sleep VERB

When you **sleep**, you close your eyes and your whole body rests.

doze
*The cat **dozed** in an armchair.*

drop off INFORMAL
*The party next door was so loud that Nora found it hard to **drop off**.*

hibernate
*Animals that are going to **hibernate** in winter have to build up their fat.*

nod off INFORMAL
*This is important. I don't want to see anyone **nodding off**.*

take a nap
*The baby has to **take a nap** after lunch or he'll cry all afternoon.*

slide VERB

When something **slides**, it moves smoothly over a surface.

glide
*The ghost **glided** over the frosty ground towards them.*

skate
*One car **skated** across the road on a patch of ice.*

skid
*Matthew **skidded** to a halt, narrowly missing the head teacher.*

slip
*Esther **slipped** in the mud and crashed to the ground.*

slither
*A snake **slithered** across their path and disappeared into the bushes.*

slippery ADJECTIVE

Something that is **slippery** is smooth, wet or greasy. It is difficult to keep hold of or to walk on.

greasy
*The door handle was so **greasy** he couldn't turn it.*

icy
*Mind how you walk on the pavement as it's very **icy**.*

oily
*Uncle Manfred's car skidded on an **oily** patch in the road.*

slimy
*Mark tried to hold the soap but it was too wet and **slimy**.*

slow ADJECTIVE

Something that is **slow** moves along without much speed.

dawdling
*Jitendra dashed past a **dawdling** crowd of nursery children.*

sluggish
*Carol's computer was old and rather **sluggish** and she wanted a new one.*

straggling
*The guide was trying to hurry a **straggling** group of tourists.*

unhurried
*Three-toed sloths made their **unhurried** way through the jungle.*

sly ADJECTIVE

Someone who is **sly** is good at tricking people in a not very nice way.

crafty
*You have to watch him because he's a **crafty** little boy.*

cunning
*She seems charming, but actually she can be quite **cunning**.*

devious
*They are **devious** when it comes to getting their own way.*

a
b
c
d
e
f
g
h
i
j
k
l
m
n
o
p
q
r
Ss
t
u
v
w
x
y
z

small

small ADJECTIVE
Something that is **small** is not as large as other things of the same kind.

little
*Alice could not get through the **little** door into the garden.*

minute
*The wizard brushed a **minute** crumb from his cloak.*

narrow
*Nathan squeezed through a **narrow** opening in the fence.*

tiny
*The doll's house was full of **tiny** furniture.*

ANTONYM: large

smart (1) ADJECTIVE
Someone who is **smart** looks neat and clean.

elegant
*The film star looked **elegant** in his designer dinner suit.*

neat
*James wore a **neat** jacket instead of his usual jumper.*

well-dressed
*When he was off-stage, the clown was always **well-dressed**.*

ANTONYM: scruffy

smart (2) ADJECTIVE
Smart can mean clever and intelligent.

bright
*Charlotte was by far the **brightest** child in her class.*

clever
*Our dog can do lots of **clever** tricks.*

intelligent
*Let's see if anyone's **intelligent** enough to solve the problem.*

sharp
*Dad thought the man was a bit too **sharp**.*

smell (1) NOUN
A **smell** is what you can sense through your nose.

aroma
*They breathed in the delicious **aroma** of new bread.*

fragrance
*Adele always chose roses for their lovely light **fragrance**.*

odour
*There was an unpleasant **odour** coming from the cave.*

scent
*Harold caught the **scent** of supper.*

stink
*At the dump, the **stink** of rotting vegetables was overpowering.*

smell (2) VERB
If something **smells**, people's noses tell them it is unpleasant.

pong INFORMAL
*"Your trainers **pong** a bit," said Grandad. "Leave them outside."*

reek
*The room **reeked** of cigarette smoke so we opened the windows.*

stink
*The chemistry lab **stank** for several days after the explosion.*

→ stink to high heaven

smile VERB

When you **smile**, the corners of your mouth move upwards, and you look happy.

beam
The baby beamed when he saw his mum.

grin
Alice saw the Cheshire cat grinning at her.

smirk
Lauren smirked at the boys. "That's where you're wrong," she said.

smooth ADJECTIVE

If something is **smooth**, it is not rough or bumpy.

silky
Holly stroked the kitten's silky fur.

sleek
Michiko envied her sister's sleek hair.

soft
The baby's skin was incredibly soft.

velvety
Moles have dark, velvety coats.

ANTONYM: rough

snatch VERB

If you **snatch** something, you take it quickly and suddenly.

grab
The boy grabbed an apple from the cart as he ran past.

grasp
The prince suddenly grasped her hand. "Please help me," he said.

seize
Robin Hood seized a stick and fought the Sheriff of Nottingham's men.

soft (1) ADJECTIVE

Something that is **soft** changes shape easily when you touch it.

downy
The owl had white downy feathers.

fluffy
Ducklings' feathers are very fluffy.

silky
The unicorn had a long, silky mane.

squashy
All those tomatoes we grew are getting a bit squashy.

ANTONYM: hard

soft (2) ADJECTIVE

A **soft** sound or voice is quiet and gentle.

gentle
My great-grandfather always speaks in gentle tones.

low
The fairy's voice was so low they could hardly hear it.

quiet
Rosaleen sang the baby to sleep with a quiet lullaby.

soft (3) ADJECTIVE

A **soft** light or colour is not too bright.

dim
In the baby's room, a dim light stays on all night.

faint
A faint rectangle of light at the window showed it was morning.

pale
Hannah chose a pale yellow colour for her bedroom walls.

ANTONYM: bright

solve

solve VERB
If you **solve** a problem, you find an answer to it.

clear up
We've got one more thing to **clear up**. Who let the cat out?

crack
It was a hard case to **crack**. The police had been working on it for weeks.

explain
"Well, that **explains** the mystery of the strange footprint," said the inspector.

get to the bottom of
Mum never **got to the bottom of** the question of the missing doughnut.

resolve
The matter was finally **resolved** when they caught the thief red-handed.

unravel
It was a fascinating puzzle and we enjoyed **unravelling** it.

work out
They tried all morning, but couldn't **work out** the riddle.

song NOUN
A **song** is a piece of music with words.

KINDS OF SONGS:

anthem	lullaby
ballad	nursery rhyme
carol	pop song
chant	rap
folk song	round
hymn	

sorry (1) ADJECTIVE
If you feel **sorry** about something, you wish you had not done it.

apologetic
Tony was **apologetic** when he broke the kitchen window.

regretful
She was **regretful** about the problems she had caused.

sorry (2) ADJECTIVE
If you feel **sorry** for someone, you feel sad for them.

full of pity
He felt **full of pity** for the sick animals at the surgery.

sad
It made Vicky **sad** to read about children without shoes.

sympathetic
Spencer felt **sympathetic** when the goalkeeper let a ball through.

sort (1) NOUN
The different **sorts** of something are the different kinds of it.

brand
Which **brand** of cereal do you have for your breakfast?

breed
A terrier is a **breed** of dog.

kind
What **kind** of animal is that?

variety
I love all **varieties** of sweets.

sort (2) VERB
If you **sort** things, you put them into groups.

arrange
Christina **arranged** all her books into alphabetical order.

grade
The eggs were **graded** according to size.

group
Children with the same interests were **grouped** into pairs.

organize
The teacher quickly **organized** them into four teams.

sound NOUN

A **sound** is something that you hear.

ANIMAL SOUNDS:

dogs:
bark whimper
growl whine
snarl yap

cats:
howl purr
mew spit
miaow

insects:
buzz murmur
hum whine

horses:
neigh
snort
whinny

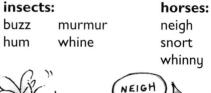

OTHER ANIMAL SOUNDS:

a bull bellows
a cow lows or moos
a donkey brays
an elephant trumpets
a frog croaks
a kookaburra laughs
a lion roars or purrs

a monkey chatters
a mouse squeaks
an owl hoots or screeches
a pig grunts or snuffles
a seagull mews or screams
a sheep bleats

SOUNDS IN AN OLD HOUSE:

doors groaning
floorboards creaking
mice skittering
shutters banging
wind howling
windows rattling

WATER SOUNDS:

a brook gurgling
a fountain playing
rain pattering or splashing
a river raging
a spring bubbling
a tap dripping
a waterfall thundering

WOODLAND SOUNDS:

birdsong
branches creaking
harsh bird cries
leaves rustling
old trees groaning
small animals scuffling
twigs cracking
wind sighing
woodpecker tapping

space

space (1) NOUN

Space is the area that is empty in a place, building or container.

capacity
The theatre had the capacity to seat a thousand people.

room
There was plenty of room round the table for the whole family.

space (2) NOUN

A **space** is a gap between two things.

distance
Measure the distance between the tables.

gap
There was a gap where Andrew had lost a tooth.

space (3) NOUN

Space is the place far above the Earth where there is no air.

MANUFACTURED OBJECTS IN SPACE:

rockets
satellites
spacecraft
space probes
space stations
space telescopes

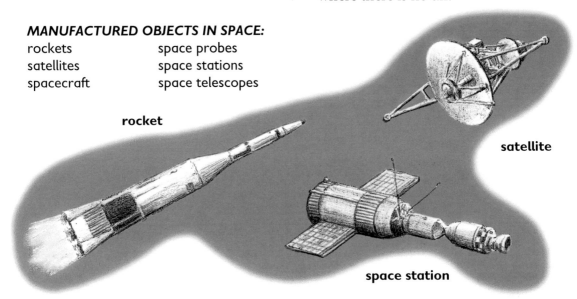

rocket

satellite

space station

NATURAL OBJECTS IN SPACE:

asteroids
comets
meteoroids
moons
planets
stars
suns

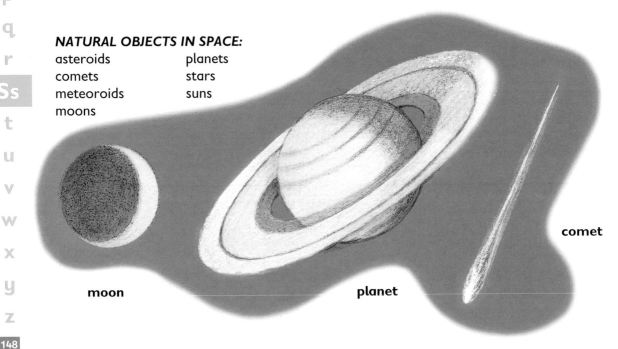

moon

planet

comet

sparkle VERB
If something **sparkles**, it shines with a lot of small bright points of light.

dance
*Julia's eyes **danced** with mischief.*

glint
*When they opened the treasure chest, jewels **glinted** in the light.*

glisten
*The sea was calm, **glistening** in the rays of the sun.*

glitter
*A diamond ring **glittered** on the princess's right hand.*

shimmer
*Her dress **shimmered** with hundreds of tiny sequins.*

twinkle
*Stars **twinkled** in the cloudless sky.*

special (1) ADJECTIVE
Something that is **special** is more important or better than other things of its kind.

extraordinary
*David had an **extraordinary** gift for imitating animals.*

important
*"This is an **important** day for everyone," said the head teacher.*

unusual
*Today there was an **unusual** feeling of excitement in the class.*

→ out of the ordinary

special (2) ADJECTIVE
Special can also mean that something is for a particular use.

particular
*The job they were doing needed a **particular** tool.*

specific
*An optician carried out a **specific** test to check Ryan's eyesight.*

spill VERB
If you **spill** something such as a liquid, you let it flow out of a container by mistake.

scatter
*Matt dropped the bucket and **scattered** seed everywhere.*

slop
*Careful! You're **slopping** milk all over the clean tablecloth.*

tip
*The baby picked up his plate and **tipped** cereal down his jumper.*

upset
*Alison waved an arm and **upset** the jug of fruit juice.*

spin VERB
When somebody or something **spins**, they turn round quickly.

revolve
*A sprinkler was **revolving** in the middle of the lawn, watering the grass.*

rotate
*Blades began to **rotate** and the helicopter roared off into the sky.*

turn
*When he gets angry he **turns** on his heel and stalks off.*

whirl
*In this scene, the ballerina **whirls** faster and faster until she becomes a white blur on the stage.*

sport

a
b
c
d
e
f
g
h
i
j
k
l
m
n
o
p
q
r
Ss
t
u
v
w
x
y
z

sport NOUN

Sports are games you play that exercise
your body.

DIFFERENT SPORTS:

baseball	skating
basketball	skiing
boxing	snooker
cricket	soccer
darts	squash
fishing	surfing
football	swimming
hockey	table tennis
netball	tennis
rugby	volleyball
running	wrestling
sailing	

basketball

surfing

sailing

skiing

snooker

squeeze

spot (1) NOUN

A **spot** is a small round mark on a surface.

blot
*His new fountain pen scattered **blots** all over the page.*

dot
*The doll was wearing a white dress with pink **dots**.*

mark
*No matter how hard he tried, he couldn't get rid of the black **mark** on his shirt.*

smudge
*You've got a **smudge** of green paint on your forehead.*

speck
*She was fussy about even the tiniest **speck** of dirt on her clothes.*

spot (2) NOUN

A **spot** can be a particular place.

location
*Our holiday cottage is in a beautiful **location** by a lake.*

place
*We need to find a good shady **place** for the picnic.*

point
*They left a small mound of stones to mark the **point** where they turned right.*

position
*They dragged their bikes to a **position** where they would not be seen.*

site
*Burned grass marked the **site** where someone had camped recently.*

spot (3) VERB

If you **spot** something, you notice it.

catch sight of
*Suddenly, they **caught sight of** a tiny man dressed in green.*

detect
*She **detected** a slight movement in the murky water.*

make out
*We **made out** a dark shape in the mist.*

see
*Let me know if you **see** anybody.*

spread VERB

If you **spread** something, you arrange it over a surface.

arrange
*They **arranged** their wet clothes on the grass to dry in the sun.*

lay out
*Chrissie proudly **laid out** her artwork on the table.*

squeeze VERB

If you **squeeze** something into a small space, you manage to fit it in.

cram
*She **crammed** the whole slice of cake into her mouth.*

crowd
*People **crowded** into the tiny room.*

jam
*He **jammed** two more books into his bag.*

pack
*"I'm sorry," said the bus driver. "I can't **pack** any more in."*

squirt

squirt VERB

If a liquid **squirts**, it comes out of a narrow opening in a thin fast stream.

shoot
*Jeremy turned the hose on his brother and **shot** water all over him.*

spout
*The fountain in the park **spouts** water ten metres in the air.*

spurt
*Diesel **spurted** from the fuel tank and the lorry had to stop.*

squeeze
*Angelica **squeezed** lemon juice into the cake mixture.*

stream
*Dad hit a pipe with a nail and water **streamed** out.*

stand (1) VERB

When you **stand**, you get to your feet and your body is upright.

get up
*He **got up** to give an old lady his seat on the bus.*

rise
*Everyone **rose** when the judge entered the law court.*

stand (2) VERB

If you **stand** something somewhere, you put it there in an upright position.

arrange
*Could you please **arrange** the dried flowers in that tall jug?*

erect
*The brothers **erected** the tent in the middle of the lawn.*

place
*Mrs Jones carefully **placed** a vase on the hall table.*

position
*Wherever she **positioned** the china figure it somehow looked odd.*

start (1) VERB

To **start** means to begin.

begin
*Reginald took up a pen and **began** to write his letter.*

commence
*"When you are quiet," snarled the professor, "I will **commence** my lecture."*

proceed
*Tim gave a small cough to get everyone's attention. Then he **proceeded** to read his poem.*

→ get under way

ANTONYM: finish

start (2) VERB

When someone **starts** something new, they create it or cause it to begin.

create
*The teenagers wanted to **create** a youth club in the village.*

establish
*Local parents were trying to **establish** a child-minding service to take care of children after school.*

introduce
*The teacher said she would **introduce** a new system next term.*

launch
*The department store has **launched** a new range of toys.*

set up
*My sister wants to **set up** a fan club for her favourite band.*

state VERB

If you **state** something, you say it clearly and formally.

announce
*Hugh **announced** he intended to be a champion tennis player one day.*

assert
*Rachel **asserted** it was her right to be in charge of the garden project.*

declare
*Sophie **declared** she would never speak to her friend again.*

say
*"It's my turn," **said** Indigo, "and that's all there is to it."*

stay VERB

If you **stay** in a place, you do not move away from it.

hang around INFORMAL
*"I'm not going to **hang around** here a moment longer," said Sebastian crossly. "I'm going home."*

linger
*Children **lingered** in the playground waiting for the coach to arrive.*

loiter
*"You mustn't **loiter** here," said the police officer firmly.*

remain
*They had to **remain** at school till their dad could fetch them.*

wait
*"**Wait** there," said Jake. "I'll just go and have a look."*

stop (1) VERB

If you **stop** what you are doing, you no longer do it.

conclude
*"I will **conclude**," said the Mayor, "with a vote of thanks."*

end
*The carousel ride **ended** after two minutes.*

finish
*Clare **finished** reading her book and went to bed.*

give up
*Dad decided to **give up** eating chocolate for a month.*

quit
*Emmanuel wanted to **quit** football and take up basketball instead.*

stop (2) VERB

To **stop** can mean to prevent something.

ban
*We were **banned** from watching TV until we'd done our homework.*

block
*Traffic on the motorway was **blocked** by a bad accident.*

hold back
*A dam **held back** the water.*

interrupt
*The teacher **interrupted** a scuffle at the back of the class.*

→ nip something in the bud

story NOUN

A **story** tells you about things that have happened. It can be about something real or something made up.

account
The teacher asked them to write an **account** of their visit to the castle.

anecdote
My uncle is full of **anecdotes** about his life in the army.

narrative
The knight told a **narrative** of his battle with the foe.

tale
Nicholas liked to read **tales** about magic and mystery.

KINDS OF STORIES:
fiction

adventure	legend
comedy	myth
crime	parable
fable	romance
fairy tale	science fiction
fantasy	thriller
ghost story	

fairy tale

non-fiction

autobiography	instructions
biography	recipe
explanation	report

strain (1) VERB

If you **strain** to do something, you try too hard.

struggle
The boys **struggled** to shift the rock, but it was hopeless.

try hard
He **tried hard** to move the old wardrobe out of the bedroom.

wrench
They **wrenched** with all their might, but the door refused to open.

strain (2) VERB

If you **strain** something like a muscle, you injure it by moving awkwardly.

damage
He **damaged** a tendon when he twisted his foot.

hurt
"You'll **hurt** yourself if you try to lift that," said his mum.

injure
The footballer **injured** a calf muscle and had to leave the field.

strange (1) ADJECTIVE

Something that is **strange** is odd or unexpected.

curious
Alice thought it **curious** that the White Rabbit had a watch.

exceptional
It was **exceptional** weather for that time of year.

extraordinary

*The spider was **extraordinary**. She'd never seen one like it before.*

funny

*Our car was making a **funny** noise, then steam came out of the engine.*

odd

*"That's **odd**," said Ellie. "I'm sure that tree wasn't there yesterday."*

peculiar

*A **peculiar** burning smell came from the witch's cauldron.*

remarkable

*They found some **remarkable** footprints in the snow.*

weird

*The children found a map with **weird** writing all over it.*

→ bizarre; mystifying

strange (2) ADJECTIVE

A **strange** place is one you have never been to before.

foreign

*He was not far from home, but the area seemed **foreign**.*

new

*While she was on holiday, Kim was happy to explore **new** towns.*

unfamiliar

*Abdullah's dog was always anxious in **unfamiliar** places.*

ANTONYM: familiar

stray VERB

If people or animals **stray**, they wander away.

be lost

*Our cat **was lost** for a week when we moved house.*

go astray

*Someone left the gate open and all the sheep **went astray**.*

straggle

*A few of the children **straggled** out into the garden.*

wander

*Samantha didn't notice she had **wandered** away from her brothers.*

strict ADJECTIVE

Someone or something **strict** must be obeyed.

firm

*The drama teacher is always very **firm** at rehearsals.*

rigid

*Victorian fathers were often **rigid** in dealing with their families.*

rigorous

*We have to follow **rigorous** rules when we are doing research.*

severe

*There were notices everywhere with **severe** warnings about trespassing.*

stern

*Our hearts sank when we saw the **stern** expression on Gran's face.*

strong (1) ADJECTIVE

If you are **strong**, you can work hard and carry heavy things.

brawny

*A **brawny** man carried their cases up four flights of stairs.*

hefty

*It took two **hefty** firemen to hold the hose that put out the fire.*

mighty

*With one **mighty** blow, the knight slew the huge dragon.*

powerful

*The woodcutter took hold of the axe in a **powerful** grip.*

tough

*Wrestlers have to be very **tough**.*

ANTONYM: weak

strong (2) ADJECTIVE

Objects or materials that are **strong** will last well.

hard-wearing

*The walkers' boots and jackets were made of **hard-wearing** material.*

heavy-duty

*The school has **heavy-duty** flooring in the sports hall.*

sturdy

*Robbie swung up on to a **sturdy** branch.*

well-built

*The castle had to be **well-built** to withstand the pounding waves.*

strong (3) ADJECTIVE

Strong can mean deeply felt.

deep

*There was a **deep** friendship between them.*

fierce

*Peter's friends knew they could count on his **fierce** loyalty.*

keen

*Jessie had a **keen** interest in all sports.*

struggle VERB

If you **struggle** to do something, you try hard to do it but find it difficult.

exert yourself

*Sayyid had to **exert himself** to be nice to his cousin.*

make every effort

*Lois **made every effort** to get in the team, but it didn't work.*

strain

*They **strained** to lift the sack, but it was too heavy.*

work hard

*The whole class **worked hard** with the history project.*

→ work like a Trojan

stubborn ADJECTIVE

Someone who is **stubborn** is determined to do what they want.

defiant

*Toby was in a **defiant** mood and refused to help clean the car.*

difficult

*Emerenzia can be **difficult** if you don't ask her nicely.*

dogged

*He won a place in the team through his **dogged** determination.*

inflexible

*Natalie is **inflexible** in her aim to become a famous writer.*

obstinate

*Her mouth was set in an **obstinate** line.*

pig-headed
*Oliver was usually too **pig-headed** to listen to anybody.*

wilful
*My sister is so **wilful** that she's always getting into trouble.*

study (1) VERB
If you **study** a subject, you spend time learning about it.

learn
*Alex went to France for the summer to **learn** the language.*

read up on
*Holly had been **reading up on** how to look after guinea pigs.*

swot INFORMAL
*Matt said he was going to have to **swot** for his exams.*

study (2) VERB
If you **study** something, you look at it carefully.

examine
*Kimberly **examined** her new science book with interest.*

investigate
*Sherlock Holmes liked to **investigate** unusual cases.*

look into
*The head teacher said she would **look into** the problem.*

research
*Scientists are always **researching** diseases and trying to find cures.*

stuffy ADJECTIVE
If a place is **stuffy**, there is not enough fresh air in it.

close
*They could hardly breathe because the air was so **close**.*

heavy
*The air was **heavy** with smoke, so the children stayed inside.*

muggy
*The **muggy** day made them all feel limp and listless.*

stale
*The air in the dragon's cave was **stale** and smelled of burning toast.*

stifling
*Great-grandma's room is always **stifling**, but that's how she likes it.*

warm
*It was so **warm** we had to fling open all the windows.*

stupid ADJECTIVE
Stupid people or ideas are not at all bright or sensible.

dim INFORMAL
*The book was so hard to read it made me feel **dim**.*

foolish
*Debbie suddenly realized it would be a **foolish** thing to do.*

half-baked
*Don't listen to his **half-baked** ideas.*

idiotic
*It's **idiotic** to go out in a boat without a life jacket.*

sudden ADJECTIVE

Something that is **sudden** happens quickly and unexpectedly.

abrupt
There was an *abrupt* change in his manner when we told him the truth.

hasty
Alex made a *hasty* exit when he saw his father's expression.

hurried
Jack's departure was *hurried.* He had spotted a giant coming towards him.

quick
After a moment, she gave a *quick* smile. "That's fine," she said.

rash
It was a *rash* decision but luckily things turned out well.

swift
With a *swift* movement, the magician produced an egg from Tony's ear.

unexpected
The prince's invitation was *unexpected*, and the lady had nothing to wear.

support (1) VERB

If you **support** someone, you want to help them.

back
At school, everyone *backs* their own team.

defend
Sarah was always ready to *defend* her friends at school.

encourage
The drama teacher *encouraged* Katie with her acting.

help
Ian's parents *helped* him a lot.

side with
In any argument, Shane always *sided with* his brother.

stand up for
Steven was quite young when he learned to *stand up for* himself.

support (2) VERB

If something **supports** an object, it holds it up firmly.

brace
Emily *braced* herself against the table.

hold up
The old lady used a forked stick to *hold up* her washing line.

prop up
Dad used lots of poles to *prop up* the tent.

reinforce
Builders *reinforced* the fence with a few concrete posts.

sure (1) ADJECTIVE

If you are **sure** something is true, you believe it is true.

certain
Kylie was *certain* she'd brought her work home, but it wasn't there.

confident
The team was *confident* it would win the game.

convinced
Both boys were *convinced* someone was following them.

positive
"Are you *positive* you gave me back that book?" she asked.

satisfied
The teacher was *satisfied* that they were telling the truth.

sure (2) ADJECTIVE

You say something is **sure** when it can be relied on.

effective
Grandma knew all sorts of effective remedies for my cold.

reliable
Looking for droppings is a reliable way of tracking animals.

surprise (1) NOUN

A **surprise** is something unexpected.

bombshell
The loss of their best goalkeeper came as a bombshell.

shock
The news that her friend was leaving was a shock to Rosie.

➔ bolt from the blue

surprise (2) NOUN

Surprise can be the way you feel about something unexpected.

amazement
Libby stared at the tiny orange fellow in amazement. "What on earth are you?" she whispered.

astonishment
Shani watched in astonishment when she saw herself on television.

wonder
They gazed in wonder at the spectacular scene before them.

surprise (3) VERB

If something **surprises** you, it gives you a feeling of surprise.

amaze
The wonderful treasures Aladdin found amazed and delighted him.

astonish
The skill of the ice skaters astonished her.

stagger
The sight of the feast spread on the table staggered him.

startle
The coldness of the sea water startled Laura.

stun
Benjamin stunned the audience with his dance performance.

swell VERB

If something **swells**, it becomes larger and rounder than usual.

bloat
He ate so much birthday cake his stomach bloated uncomfortably.

bulge
The ogre's belly bulged over his belt.

get bigger
Mr Jones measured the pumpkins every day, willing them to get bigger.

grow
Before his horrified eyes, the toad grew to an enormous size.

a
b
c
d
e
f
g
h
i
j
k
l
m
n
o
p
q
r
Ss
t
u
v
w
x
y
z

Tt

take (1) VERB

If you **take** something, you put your hand round it and carry it.

carry
Let me carry your books for you.

clasp
Katherine clasped the baby in her arms.

grip
"Grip the handle with both hands. This bag is heavy," said my cousin.

hold
He offered to hold her coat while she looked in her bag.

take (2) VERB

If someone **takes** you somewhere, you go there with them.

bring
You can bring a friend to the party if you want to.

guide
"I'll guide you on the first part of the journey," said the wizard.

lead
Spot led Julia to his favourite park.

take (3) VERB

If a person **takes** something that does not belong to them, they steal it.

grab
Alexander grabbed an apple from his neighbour's tree.

snatch
The thief snatched a diamond ring and ran from the shop.

steal
Thomas saw an old man steal a book and slip out of the back door.

talent NOUN

Talent is the natural ability a person has to do something well.

ability
Charlotte was featured on TV because of her musical ability.

aptitude
Kerena has an aptitude for working with little children.

flair
Jeremy showed a flair for drawing when he was very young.

genius
Ms Kent's genius as a teacher makes her lessons exciting.

gift
My grandad has a gift for making people feel confident.

knack
"It takes a special knack to build these model kits," Simon said.

skill
The children admired the conjuror's skill.

talk (1) VERB

When you **talk**, you say things to someone.

chat
*My sister can **chat** on the phone for hours.*

converse
*We are learning to **converse** in French.*

gossip
*Old men would stand **gossiping** on the corner all day.*

prattle
*Tom couldn't stop **prattling** about his summer holiday.*

speak
*Tony had plenty to say, but they wouldn't let him **speak**.*

talk (2) NOUN

A **talk** is an informal speech.

address
*The head teacher gave a short **address** welcoming the parents.*

lecture
*The professor's **lecture** was about endangered wild animals.*

report
*Robert gave a detailed **report** on the football match.*

sermon
*The vicar's **sermon** was a bit long.*

speech
*There was a **speech** before the prizes were given out.*

tall ADJECTIVE

Something **tall** is higher than average.

giant
*A **giant** statue stood in the park.*

high
*Charles lived on the top floor of a **high** block of flats.*

lanky
*A **lanky** young man played music for them on his guitar.*

soaring
*They gazed up from the beach at **soaring** white cliffs.*

towering
*Joe found himself in a sunny clearing surrounded by **towering** trees.*

ANTONYM: short

tame ADJECTIVE

A **tame** animal is not afraid of humans and will not hurt them.

docile
*Some pet parrots can be a bit vicious, but Sam's is really **docile**.*

domesticated
***Domesticated** animals help humans in lots of ways.*

gentle
*Most pets are **gentle** and easy to handle.*

obedient
*However **obedient** that elephant seems, it's still dangerous.*

ANTONYM: wild

a
b
c
d
e
f
g
h
i
j
k
l
m
n
o
p
q
r
s
Tt
u
v
w
x
y
z

taste

taste (1) NOUN

The **taste** of something is the flavour of it.

flavour
*I love the **flavour** of strawberry jam.*

tang
*The sharp **tang** of lemon is refreshing.*

taste (2) NOUN

If you have a **taste** of food or drink, you try a small amount of it.

bit
*I'll try a little **bit**, but I don't think I'll like it.*

bite
*"Can I have a **bite** of your burger too?" asked Dee, as she reached for a chip.*

drop
*George pestered Grandpa for a **drop** of his hot tea.*

morsel
*Mum gave the baby a **morsel** of egg to see if he would eat it.*

mouthful
*One **mouthful** of the soup was enough.*

nibble
*Jeremy handed him a broken piece of biscuit. "There's only a **nibble** left," he said.*

sip
*"Just a **sip**," she pleaded.*

spoonful
*The cook had a **spoonful** of the stew, and smiled. "That's fine," she said.*

tear VERB

If you **tear** something, such as paper or fabric, you pull it apart.

claw
*"Don't let the kitten **claw** a hole in your new jumper," said Auntie.*

divide
***Divide** the paper in half and give one piece to your partner.*

ladder
*Mum keeps on **laddering** her stockings on that chair.*

rip
*He didn't want to **rip** his new jeans on the barbed wire.*

scratch
*Nick didn't mean to **scratch** the wallpaper when he parked his bike in the hall.*

shred
*At the end of the story, Naomi **shreds** the letter into little pieces and bursts into tears.*

slit
*Josh was eager to **slit** open the envelope.*

split
*"The ship's sail could **split** in this weather," warned the sailor.*

tease VERB

To **tease** means to make fun of someone, or annoy them.

annoy
*Stop **annoying** your sister.*

badger
*The boys wouldn't stop **badgering** her till she agreed to go with them.*

make fun of
*It's cruel to **make fun of** people.*

pester
*If you keep **pestering** me, we won't go out at all.*

torment
*That cat will scratch you if you don't stop **tormenting** her.*

→ aggravate; needle

terrible

tell (1) VERB

If you **tell** someone something, you let them know about it.

inform
*He phoned the police to **inform** them of the burglary.*

mention
*Please don't **mention** this to anybody.*

reveal
*My friend spoilt the book by **revealing** the surprise ending.*

say
*He wouldn't **say** what he had been doing.*

warn
*It's the weather forecaster's job to **warn** us of possible flooding.*

tell (2) VERB

If someone **tells** you to do something, they say you must do it.

command
*The troops were **commanded** to move forward at dawn.*

direct
*The police officer **directed** them to leave the building immediately.*

instruct
*The pirate captain **instructed** his men to hide the treasure.*

order
*"I can't **order** you to exercise," said Dr Foster, "but it will be good for your health."*

tender ADJECTIVE

Someone who is **tender** shows gentle and caring feelings.

gentle
*My uncle's a **gentle** person who would never hurt anyone.*

kind
*Julia has a **kind** mother who comforts her when she's upset.*

loving
*Grandma gave him a **loving** kiss when they met.*

soft-hearted
*Mum is always **soft-hearted** when it comes to small animals.*

terrible ADJECTIVE

Something **terrible** is serious and unpleasant.

alarming
*An **alarming** scream ripped through the icy forest.*

appalling
*There was an **appalling** accident on the foggy motorway.*

awful
*They wrinkled their noses at the **awful** smell of burning.*

bad
*The witch made a **bad** mistake when she recited the spell.*

dreadful
***Dreadful** weather nearly ruined Natalie's birthday party.*

horrible
*A **horrible** ogre stole all the sheep.*

test

test (1) VERB

If someone **tests** something, they try to find out what it is like.

check
They **checked** the ground carefully before putting their weight on it.

examine
Scientists **examined** the water and declared it was pure.

investigate
Birdwatchers are **investigating** the way falcons hunt for food.

research
In class we are **researching** different ways of growing plants.

try
Amy **tried** the yo-yo before she decided to buy it.

try out
Josh **tried out** his new pen.

test (2) NOUN

A **test** is an attempt to find out how good somebody or something is.

check
Douglas went to the clinic for a full health **check**.

exam
My sister did really well in her **exam**.

examination
Some parts of the plane were taken away for **examination** purposes.

trial
Scientists were carrying out **trials** on new medication for colds.

thick (1) ADJECTIVE

An object that is **thick** is deeper through than other things of the same kind.

deep
Deep layers of mud lay by the river.

fat
Melanie chose a nice **fat** book to read.

solid
A **solid** carpet of snow covered the fields.

wide
A **wide** privet hedge protected them from the traffic.

ANTONYM: thin

thick (2) ADJECTIVE

Thick liquids do not flow easily.

concentrated
The fruit juice was so **concentrated** she could stand her straw up in it.

condensed
Mum added water to the **condensed** soup.

thick (3) ADJECTIVE

Thick can mean grouped closely together.

bristling
Grandfather has a **bristling** moustache.

dense
The children were lost in a **dense** forest.

luxuriant
A maid brushed the princess's long, **luxuriant** hair.

things

thin (1) ADJECTIVE

A **thin** person weighs less than most people of the same height.

bony
The wizard's old cloak hung limply on his bony shoulders.

lean
The cowboy was as lean and as tough as his horse.

scrawny
A scrawny dog came into the garden.

slender
The girl modelling the clothes was tall, dark and slender.

slim
Mum has managed to keep her slim figure.

ANTONYM: fat

thin (2) ADJECTIVE

Something that is **thin** measures a small distance from side to side.

fine
The baby's head was covered in fine hairs.

flimsy
One of the fairies wore a dress of strange, flimsy material.

light
Light curtains hung at the window.

narrow
The witch's nose was long and narrow.

sparse
A sparse beard was sprouting on his chin.

ANTONYM: thick

thin (3) ADJECTIVE

Thin liquids are weak and watery.

runny
The pancake mixture was too runny.

watery
Oliver said the soup was too watery.

weak
The jelly was too weak to set properly.

thing NOUN

A **thing** is an object, rather than an animal or a human being.

article
His case burst open and articles were scattered all over the floor.

device
They looked for a device to help them reach their kite. It was stuck high up in a tree.

item
There were lots of items on the list that they still had to pack.

object
The antique shop had several interesting objects for sale.

things PLURAL NOUN

Your **things** are your clothes or possessions.

baggage
They had to wait to collect their baggage at the airport.

belongings
The man was poor, and had very few personal belongings.

bits and pieces
Gather your bits and pieces and put them away tidily.

equipment
Dad loaded the camping equipment into the trailer.

gear
We took our swimming gear with us to the beach.

luggage
When we went on holiday, we filled our roof rack with luggage.

possessions
The film showed people with their possessions piled up in carts.

stuff
My cousin had a lot of stuff with him when he came to stay.

165

think

think (1) VERB

When you **think**, you use your mind to consider ideas or problems.

consider
You need to consider carefully what you should do.

estimate
I estimate the whole journey will take about four hours.

imagine
Ben tried to imagine how he would feel.

wonder
Do you ever wonder what it would be like to be a bird?

think (2)

If you **think** something is true, you believe it is true but you are not sure.

believe
Sam believed his parents were planning a holiday.

feel
Daisy felt she might have won a prize.

guess
We guess our teacher is going to get married soon.

reckon
"I reckon it's going to snow tonight," said Grandad.

suppose
I suppose I should get on with my work.

understand
We understand there's going to be a new doctor at the surgery.

thoughtful ADJECTIVE

A **thoughtful** person remembers what other people want or need, and tries to be kind to them.

attentive
We like that restaurant. The food is good and the staff are attentive.

caring
He's a caring boy who helps his mum.

considerate
Dad's boss is considerate. She doesn't mind him being late when he takes us all to school.

helpful
Sara took a helpful friend when she went to choose a book for her mum.

kind
"How kind of you to fetch my wand," said the wizard.

unselfish
Tom is really unselfish. He would even give you his last sweet.

throw VERB

If you **throw** an object that you are holding, you send it through the air.

fling
Joel flung his jacket on the bed.

hurl
Natalie burst into tears and hurled her book across the room.

sling
She slung her bag over one shoulder and dashed to the car.

toss
They went into the park and tossed sticks for the dog.

thrust VERB

If you **thrust** something somewhere, you push or move it there quickly with a lot of force.

force
He **forced** the key into the lock and the door swung open.

push
Lara **pushed** the secret note into the pocket of her jeans.

shove
We **shoved** our swimming things in a bag and ran to the beach.

tidy ADJECTIVE

Something that is **tidy** is neat and well arranged.

neat
Everything about him is so **neat** he looks as if he never relaxes.

orderly
The top of her desk looks **orderly**, but the drawers are in a dreadful muddle.

smart
The police looked **smart** in their uniforms.

straight
They all worked hard and the room was **straight** in no time.

trim
Grandpa likes to have **trim** flowerbeds.

uncluttered
The house was so **uncluttered** it didn't look like a real home.

ANTONYM: untidy

tie (1) VERB

If you **tie** an object to something, you fasten it with something like string.

bind
They **bound** the sticks in small bundles to make them easy to carry.

fasten
The latch had broken, so Daniel **fastened** the gate with a piece of wire.

knot
The magician **knotted** scarves together, then turned them into a rabbit.

lash
They **lashed** planks together with rope to make a raft.

secure
Dad **secured** the luggage on the car before we went on holiday.

tether
He **tethered** the donkey to a strong post.

tie (2) VERB

If two people or teams **tie**, they have the same score.

be level
In the competition the two boys **were level**.

be neck and neck
They **were neck and neck** across the finish line and everyone cheered.

draw
"After an exciting game, the two teams **drew**," he said.

time

time NOUN

Time is what is measured in seconds, minutes, hours, days and years.

MEASURING TIME:

second	
minute	60 seconds
hour	60 minutes
day	24 hours
week	7 days
fortnight	14 days
lunar month	28 days
year	365 days
leap year	366 days
decade	10 years
century	100 years
millennium	1000 years

DAYS OF THE WEEK:

Monday	Friday
Tuesday	Saturday
Wednesday	Sunday
Thursday	

NUMBER OF DAYS IN THE MONTH:

January	31
February	28 (or 29 in a leap year)
March	31
April	30
May	31
June	30
July	31
August	31
September	30
October	31
November	30
December	31

TIMES OF DAY:

dawn	noon	evening
morning	afternoon	night
midday	dusk	midnight

SEASONS:

spring	autumn
summer	winter

spring

summer

autumn

winter

HOW OFTEN:

always	sometimes
never	twice
often	usually
once	

MORE TIME WORDS:

now	tomorrow
today	yesterday

tiny ADJECTIVE

Something that is **tiny** is very small.

little

*A **little** spider scuttled across Kylie's desk.*

microscopic

*He flicked a **microscopic** speck of dust from his jacket.*

miniature

*Ellie kept a **miniature** portrait of her great-grandmother on her dressing table.*

minute

*All I had to eat was a **minute** helping of cottage pie.*

small

*The shoes were **small** enough to fit a doll.*

ANTONYM: huge

tip (1) NOUN

The **tip** of something long and narrow is the end of it.

end

*The **end** of the cat's tail began to twitch in annoyance.*

peak

*Mist covered the **peak** of the mountain, so they decided not to go up.*

point

*Georgia likes to keep a sharp **point** on her pencils.*

top

*The **top** of an iceberg is always much smaller than the part below the water line.*

tip (2) VERB

If you **tip** an object, you move it so that it is no longer straight.

lean

*Robert **leaned** his chair back and almost lost his balance.*

overturn

*The boat **overturned** and they all fell into the water.*

spill

*Nina **spilled** her juice all over the table and chair.*

tilt

*If you **tilt** that jug any further you'll lose the lot.*

tired ADJECTIVE

If you are **tired**, you feel that you want to rest or sleep.

exhausted

*We were **exhausted** after climbing every tower in the castle.*

ready to drop

*By the time Patrick had walked ten miles he was **ready to drop**.*

sleepy

*At bedtime the baby yawned and gave her mum a **sleepy** smile.*

worn out

*Layla was too **worn out** to argue.*

→ absolutely shattered; cream-crackered; dead on your feet

tool

a
b
c
d
e
f
g
h
i
j
k
l
m
n
o
p
q
r
s
Tt
u
v
w
x
y
z

tool NOUN

A **tool** is anything that you use to help you do something.

device

It's a **device** that sailors used to find their position at sea.

gadget

We need a **gadget** to hold these two bits together while they stick.

instrument

My dad has an **instrument** for measuring things really accurately.

utensil

You can't even begin this sort of cookery without a rack full of **utensils**.

top (1) NOUN

The **top** of something is its highest point, part or surface.

crest

A man on a surfboard appeared on the **crest** of a wave.

head

Rachel wrote her name and the date at the **head** of the page.

peak

Holiday firms tend to charge **peak** prices during summer.

summit

The **summit** of the mountain was covered in snow.

tip

The **tips** of the pine trees were hidden in thick mist.

top (2) NOUN

The **top** of a bottle, jar or tube is its cap or lid.

cap

Lewis poured himself a drink and put the **cap** back on the bottle.

lid

The **lid** of the jam jar rolled off the table and clattered on the floor.

touch (1) VERB

If you **touch** something, you feel it with your hand.

feel

Chloe **felt** the parcel to try to guess what was in it.

handle

Don't forget to wash your hands after you've **handled** the hamster.

pat

Jason **patted** the dog's head and stroked its soft coat.

rub

"Yum, yum!" said the ogre, **rubbing** his rounded stomach.

stroke

The cat came over to me and demanded to be **stroked**.

touch (2) VERB

If two things are **touching**, there is no space between them.

brush

His fingers accidentally **brushed** the wet paint and smudged it.

graze

"A bullet has **grazed** this soldier's arm," said the nurse.

meet

Branches **met** overhead, casting deep shadows on the road.

travel VERB

When you **travel**, you go from one place to another.

go

The family is **going** to India for a holiday this year.

make your way

Some of the hikers were planning to **make their way** up the mountain.

take a trip

Grandma wants to **take a trip** in a hot-air balloon this summer.

tree NOUN

A **tree** is a large plant with a woody trunk, branches and leaves.

KINDS OF TREES:

ash	oak
beech	palm
birch	pine
fir	poplar
holly	sycamore
horse chestnut	willow
larch	yew
maple	

maple

oak

palm

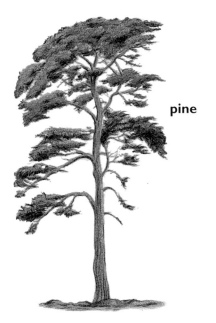

pine

willow

trick

trick (1) NOUN

A **trick** is something that deceives someone.

con INFORMAL
A letter claimed we could make lots of money, but it was a con.

deception
The deception worked and the man thought he had won a new car.

hoax
An ambulance rushed to the scene and discovered that the call was a stupid hoax.

trick (2) VERB

If a person **tricks** someone, they deceive them.

cheat
A wicked man cheated Michael's father out of some land he owned.

con INFORMAL
Last week someone conned my aunt out of her holiday savings.

deceive
Someone tried to deceive Mum by claiming he was her cousin.

fool
Jack fooled Harry into clearing up the paints in the classroom.

trickle VERB

When a liquid **trickles**, it flows slowly in small amounts.

dribble
Saliva sometimes dribbles from the baby's mouth when he's teething.

leak
Water was leaking from the kitchen tap into the sink.

ooze
Mud oozed up between her toes as she walked barefoot across the field.

seep
There were damp patches on the ceiling where rain was seeping through the roof.

trip (1) VERB

If you **trip**, you catch your foot on something and fall over.

fall
Darcy spun round quickly and fell over a paving stone.

stumble
The track was rough and they stumbled several times.

tumble
Kylie tumbled over a toy, banged her head and started to cry.

trip (2) NOUN

A **trip** is a journey to a place and back again.

day out
We were looking forward to a day out in the country.

excursion
The class went on an excursion to the Roman ruins.

jaunt
A large notice offered cut-price jaunts in a riverboat.

journey
It was a long journey and the boys were very tired.

outing
She wanted more books to read, so they went on an outing to the library.

voyage
Tallulah hoped the sea would be calm for the voyage.

trouble (1) NOUN

Trouble is something that worries or bothers you.

bother
*Ellie had a bit of **bother** at school when she lost her glasses.*

difficulty
*They had some **difficulty** in finding the right place.*

hassle INFORMAL
*"I really don't need this **hassle** today," complained the zoo keeper.*

problem
*The **problem** was finding somewhere to practise his violin.*

trouble (2) VERB

If you **trouble** somebody, you bother them.

annoy
*Junk mail **annoys** my parents. They say it is a waste of paper.*

bother
*"Don't **bother** that cat or she'll scratch you." said Auntie Mavis.*

disturb
*It wasn't a good idea to **disturb** the wasps.*

irritate
*It **irritates** Mum if I forget to say "please" and "thank you".*

pester
*Stop **pestering** me. I'm not going to change my mind.*

worry
*Andrew was **worried** by the thought of his tree house blowing down in the storm.*

true ADJECTIVE

A **true** story or statement is based on facts and is not made up.

accurate
*They were able to give an **accurate** description of the burglar.*

correct
*This time, give me the **correct** version of the story.*

factual
*I want a **factual** report. Don't make anything up.*

genuine
*Tales of the explorer's life in the jungle are quite **genuine**.*

real
*The TV programme showed the **real** problems of being a star.*

trust VERB

If you **trust** someone, you believe that they are honest and will not do anything to hurt you.

believe
*You can always **believe** what he says.*

count on
*Can I **count on** you to back me up?*

depend on
*On an adventure like this, you need a friend you can **depend on**.*

rely on
*Now she's ill she has to **rely on** her neighbours to do the shopping.*

try

try (1) VERB

If you **try** to do something, you do your best to do it.

aim
Andrew **aimed** to catch a big fish for supper, and he did it too!

attempt
Mehmet is going to **attempt** the high jump one more time.

do your best
Gary is not very good at woodwork, but he **does his best**.

make an effort
If Marcus **made an effort** he could do really well.

struggle
The girls **struggled** to open the door, but it was stuck fast.

→ have a go; have a crack; have a shot

try (2) VERB

If you **try** something, you test it to see what it is like.

check out
Granville wanted to **check out** the new computer game.

sample
We decided to **sample** one of Mum's delicious fairy cakes.

taste
"Just **taste** it," said the chef. "You might find you like it."

test
The mechanic **tested** the engine and the brakes on our car.

turn (1) NOUN

If people take **turns** to do something, they do it one after the other.

chance
I'm sure I can do it. Just give me a **chance**.

go
That's not fair! It's my **go**!

shot
At last Mark was allowed to have a **shot**.

try
"Let me have a **try**," said Grandma. "I used to be good at this."

turn (2) VERB

When someone or something **turns**, they change direction.

bend
At the top of the hill, trees **bent** away from the wind.

spin
Lauren **spun** round when she heard the door open.

swivel
Our TV is on a bracket so that you can **swivel** it.

twirl
Floella **twirled** around for her mum to admire the dress.

wind
The hillside track **wound** back on itself several times.

turn into VERB

When something **turns into** something else, it becomes that thing.

become
*When water freezes, it **becomes** ice.*

change into
*Caterpillars **change into** butterflies or moths.*

develop into
*Tadpoles soon **develop into** frogs.*

transform into
*With the help of some wings, Rachel was **transformed into** a fairy.*

twist (1) VERB

When you **twist** something, you turn one end in the opposite direction to the other.

coil
*The sailor **coiled** the rope carefully as she got ready to leave.*

curl
*Natalie spent ages **curling** her hair into attractive shapes.*

loop
*The farmer **looped** some wire round the gate to keep it shut.*

turn
*Florence **turned** the handle and pulled the door open.*

wind
*Dad **wound** string round and round the broken chair leg.*

twist (2) VERB

When something **twists**, it moves or bends into a strange shape.

bend
*Sophie's foot slipped on a rock and her ankle **bent** painfully.*

curve
*The road **curved** to the left and suddenly we saw the cottage.*

weave
*Branches of trees **weaved** above our heads, making a shady tunnel.*

wind
*A narrow stream **wound** through the countryside between green meadows.*

zigzag
*Halfway down the mountainside the track **zigzagged**, slowing the car right down.*

typical ADJECTIVE

Something that is **typical** is what you would expect.

average
*An **average** woman needs about 2000 calories a day.*

normal
*For us, a **normal** day starts at 7a.m.*

standard
*His **standard** way of dealing with problems is to ignore them.*

usual
*It was Margaret's **usual** Wednesday visit to the hairdresser.*

Wednesday

a
b
c
d
e
f
g
h
i
j
k
l
m
n
o
p
q
r
s
Tt
u
v
w
x
y
z

Uu

ugly ADJECTIVE

Someone or something that is **ugly** is not pleasant to look at.

hideous
*The ogre gave them a **hideous** grin.*

repulsive
*Christopher opened his present and found a **repulsive** jumper.*

unattractive
*The troll was **unattractive** to say the least.*

→ not much to look at

understand (1) VERB

If you **understand** someone, you know what they mean.

follow
*It was so complicated they couldn't **follow** it at all.*

get
*The others were laughing, but Tom didn't **get** the joke.*

see
*It was difficult, but we soon **saw** what he was getting at.*

take in
*The teacher had to tell her three times before she **took it in**.*

understand (2) VERB

If you **understand** something, you know how or why it is happening.

appreciate
*When they tried ice-skating they **appreciated** how difficult it was.*

fathom
*It's hard to **fathom** how ants communicate, but they do.*

grasp
*Anthony had only just **grasped** how a tin-opener worked.*

realize
*Vicky soon **realized** that nursing is a demanding job.*

understand (3) VERB

To **understand** can mean to hear of something.

believe
*I **believe** you're going up next year?*

gather
*They **gathered** that a new teacher was joining the school.*

hear
*Mum **heard** a new supermarket was opening soon.*

unhappy ADJECTIVE

Someone who is **unhappy** is sad or miserable.

depressed
*He felt **depressed** when he failed the music exam.*

down
*She was feeling **down** about having to move away from her friends.*

miserable
*Dad said he'd had a **miserable** day at work and was glad to be home.*

sad
*They were all **sad** that Great-grandma wasn't well enough to come to the party.*

ANTONYM: happy

upset (1) ADJECTIVE

If you are **upset**, you are unhappy or disappointed.

distressed
*Miss Muffet was **distressed** when a spider sat down beside her.*

hurt
*Sergei was **hurt** when his sister laughed at him.*

troubled
*My friend seemed **troubled**, so I put an arm round his shoulders.*

unhappy
*Sophie was **unhappy** because her kitten wasn't well.*

upset (2) VERB

If you **upset** someone, you make them worried or unhappy.

bother
*I don't want to **bother** Grandma just now.*

distress
*David was sorry he had **distressed** his Auntie Jo.*

upset (3) VERB

If someone **upsets** something, they turn it over by accident.

knock over
*Nina stumbled against a table and **knocked over** a vase.*

spill
*A toddler **spilt** orange juice right over her homework.*

useful ADJECTIVE

If something is **useful**, it helps you in some way.

handy
*Mum said it would be **handy** to have a robot that did housework.*

helpful
*Robert was given a **helpful** book on camping and some insect repellent.*

practical
*"That rucksack isn't **practical** for hiking," said Dan. "It's too small."*

valuable
*The first-aid box was a **valuable** part of their luggage.*

useless ADJECTIVE

If it is **useless** to do something, it will not achieve anything helpful.

fruitless
*Their search for the missing spade was **fruitless**, and they had to give up.*

futile
*She had a **futile** argument with her dad about staying out late.*

hopeless
*It was **hopeless** trying to work with such poor tools.*

pointless
*"This is a **pointless** discussion," said Mum. "You're not going and that's the end of it."*

ANTONYM: **useful**

Vv

vague ADJECTIVE

Things that are **vague** are not definite or clear.

dim
*When he woke, Marty had only a **dim** memory of the frightening dream.*

general
*He gave a **general** outline of the project and left us to work out the details.*

hazy
*Mrs Jefferson could give only a **hazy** description of the burglar.*

woolly
*His account of the holiday in Spain was rather **woolly**.*

vain ADJECTIVE

A **vain** person is too proud of how they look or what they can do.

boastful
*Spencer didn't mind sounding **boastful** about his adventures.*

conceited
*I don't want Emma for a friend. She's far too **conceited**.*

proud
*He's too **proud** to admit that he might be wrong.*

valuable (1) ADJECTIVE

Things that are **valuable** are worth a lot of money.

expensive
*Calvin's parents gave him an **expensive** mountain bike.*

precious
*The princess's hand sparkled with **precious** diamonds and emeralds.*

valuable (2) ADJECTIVE

Help or advice that is **valuable** is very useful.

helpful
*Advice from older people can be **helpful**.*

important
*The coach gave her some **important** tips to help improve her swimming.*

useful
*He has lots of **useful** ideas about how to keep plants healthy.*

worthwhile
*The teacher helped him with some **worthwhile** guidance on his project.*

variety (1) NOUN

A **variety** of things is a number of different kinds.

assortment
*There was an **assortment** of biscuits still in the tin.*

collection
*The family had a huge **collection** of books on shelves around the room.*

mixture
*I like to have a **mixture** of chocolates.*

range
*The shop sold a **range** of shampoos.*

variety (2) NOUN

A **variety** is a particular type of something.

class
*There are several different **classes** of butterfly here.*

kind
*She couldn't decide what **kind** of rose to plant by the gate.*

sort
*We've got lots of different apples. Which **sort** do you like best?*

type
*How quickly a plant grows depends on what **type** it is.*

vegetable NOUN

Vegetables are plants, or parts of plants, that can be eaten.

SOME VEGETABLES:

asparagus
aubergine
  (also known as eggplant)
beans
cabbage
carrot
cauliflower
chilli
courgette
  (also known as zucchini)
leek
marrow
mushroom

onion
parsnip
peas
pepper
  (also known as capsicum)
potato
pumpkin
spinach
sprouts
squash
sweet potato
turnip
yam

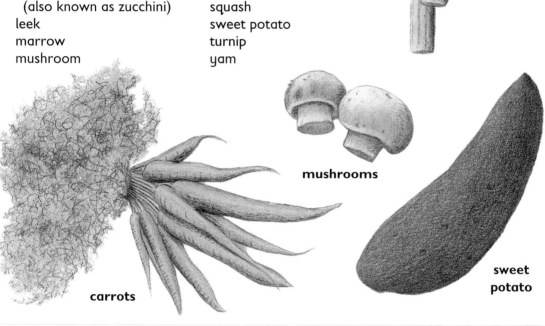

asparagus

mushrooms

sweet
potato

carrots

version NOUN

A **version** of something is a form of it in which some details are different from other forms.

account
*Esther's **account** of the holiday was very different from Charlie's.*

description
*Everyone gave a different **description** of the accident.*

story
*The teacher didn't know whose **story** she should believe.*

victory NOUN

A **victory** is a success in a battle or competition.

success
*Supporters cheered the team for its **success** in the match.*

triumph
*The slaying of the fearsome dragon was a **triumph** for the knight.*

win
*The swimming team had never been beaten and was confident it would have another **win**.*

a
b
c
d
e
f
g
h
i
j
k
l
m
n
o
p
q
r
s
t
u
Vv
w
x
y
z

wait VERB

If you **wait**, you spend time before something happens.

hang on
Hang on! I've got to get my coat.

hold on
*His friends couldn't **hold on** any longer, so they went on ahead.*

stay
*The dog had to **stay** outside the shop.*

walk VERB

When you **walk**, you move along by putting one foot in front of the other.

creep
*They **crept** silently past the sleeping dog.*

dawdle
*The children **dawdled** along the path.*

hike
*Rupert **hiked** for five miles in the hills.*

limp
*One of the elves was **limping** awkwardly.*

march
*Evelyn **marched** along the road in time to the music.*

prowl
*He saw a wolf **prowling** around nearby.*

wander VERB

If you **wander**, you walk around without going in any particular direction.

drift
*We **drifted** from shop to shop without buying anything.*

ramble
*The boys enjoyed **rambling** over the hills, collecting blackberries.*

roam
*Our cat likes to **roam** in the fields and play in the long grass.*

stray
*"Make sure you shut the gates," said the farmer, "or the sheep will **stray**."*

want (1) VERB

If you **want** something, you wish for it.

desire
*The knight **desired** to marry the king's clever daughter.*

fancy
*Mum really **fancied** an iced bun.*

wish for
*Latasha's cousin was given all the things she could possibly **wish for**.*

want (2) VERB

To **want** something can mean to need it for some reason.

be short of
*They discovered they **were short of** dry firewood for the stove.*

need
*Alex's hair **needed** cutting. He could hardly see where he was going.*

require
*An old lady **required** help to get across the busy road.*

warm (1) ADJECTIVE

Something that is **warm** has some heat, but not enough to be hot.

comfortable
*His room in the hospital was kept at a **comfortable** temperature.*

cosy
*Mark felt **cosy** under the duvet.*

not too hot
*Daisy's cocoa was **not too hot**.*

snug
*Raju was **snug** in his winter gear.*

warm (2) ADJECTIVE

Someone who is **warm** is friendly and affectionate.

affectionate
*Desdemona gave her grandmother an **affectionate** hug.*

cheerful
*That lady in the sweetshop is always **cheerful** and friendly.*

friendly
*The policeman gave her a **friendly** smile.*

kindly
*Our school janitor is a **kindly** person.*

loving
*Christopher wrote **loving** messages in the birthday card.*

pleasant
*You can be sure of a **pleasant** welcome in Kate's house.*

watch (1) VERB

If you **watch** something, you look at it carefully to see what happens.

gaze at
*Hannah **gazed at** the butterfly as it sipped nectar from the flower.*

look at
*Robert wanted to **look at** the cricket match on the green.*

observe
*The magician told them to **observe** him very carefully.*

see
*They tried to **see** the way the machine worked, but it was too complicated.*

stare at
*We **stared at** a spider making its web.*

watch (2) VERB

To **watch** can mean to look after something.

guard
*The dog could be relied on to **guard** the house when they were out.*

keep an eye on
*Charlotte promised to **keep an eye on** the baby while Mum was upstairs.*

look after
*Could you please **look after** the cat while we're out?*

mind
*Danny offered to **mind** the shop for half an hour.*

take care of
*A neighbour **took care of** the children for the afternoon.*

a
b
c
d
e
f
g
h
i
j
k
l
m
n
o
p
q
r
s
t
u
v
Ww
x
y
z

water

NOUN

Water is a clear liquid that all living things need in order to live.

LARGE AREAS OF WATER:
lake   reservoir
ocean   sea

SMALL AREAS OF WATER:
pond   puddle
pool

WATER FLOWING BETWEEN BANKS:
brook   river
canal   stream

FALLING WATER:
cascade   waterfall
cataract weir

RACING WATER:
rapids

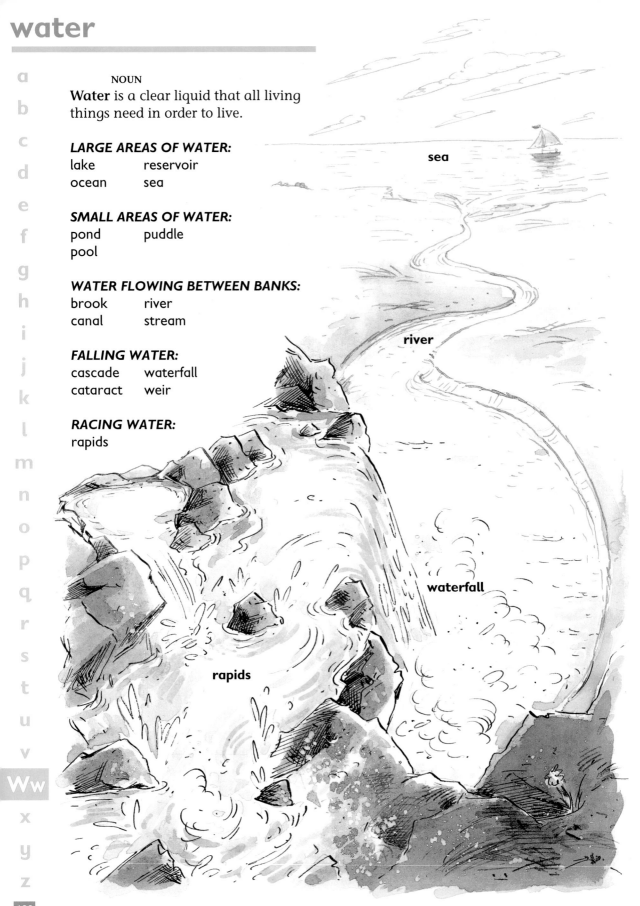

sea

river

waterfall

rapids

way (1) NOUN

The **way** to a particular place is the direction you have to go to get there.

direction
We turned left, but soon found it was the wrong direction.

lane
"I'm sure this is the right lane," Graham said at last.

path
They came to a fork and weren't sure which path to choose.

road
"Is this the road to the Town Hall?" asked Dick importantly.

route
Dad was so keen to try out his brand-new car that he drove the long route to Granny's house.

track
The track to the farm was easy to find, but it was very muddy.

way (2) NOUN

A **way** of doing something is how it can be done.

fashion
"We'll never do it if we carry on in this fashion," said Dad.

manner
Albert approached every problem in a calm manner.

means
They tried every means they could think of to get him out of bed.

method
There were several methods of doing it. Sophie chose the simplest.

system
"This system will work," said Tom. "Just give it a chance."

technique
The plumber showed us a technique to stop the leak.

weak (1) ADJECTIVE

People or animals that are **weak** do not have much strength or energy.

delicate
Louise was delicate as a young child.

feeble
Mum said she was feeling much too feeble to go swimming.

frail
The old man was too frail to carry his shopping home.

puny
Sita chose the puniest puppy of the litter.

sickly
"Actually I feel rotten," said Ben, and gave a sickly smile.

ANTONYM: **strong**

weak (2) ADJECTIVE

If an object or part of an object is **weak**, it could break easily.

flimsy
The boat looked too flimsy to take the whole family.

fragile
Ranjit's new toy was so fragile it broke in the first ten minutes.

rickety
The chair looked nice, but one of the legs was rickety.

ANTONYM: **strong**

weak (3) ADJECTIVE

Drinks that are **weak** do not have a strong taste.

diluted
Lizzie complained that her orange squash was too diluted.

tasteless
The tea in the cafe was tasteless.

thin
The tomato soup was so thin it was more like water.

a
b
c
d
e
f
g
h
i
j
k
l
m
n
o
p
q
r
s
t
u
v
Ww
x
y
z

weather

weather NOUN

The **weather** is what it is like outside, for example raining, sunny or windy.

WEATHER WORDS: ADJECTIVES

changeable weather
breezy	showery

cold weather
bitter	freezing	icy
cold	frosty	snowy

dull weather
chilly	cool	foggy
cloudy	drizzly	misty

stormy weather
thundery	windy

sunny weather
bright	fine	sunny
clear	hot	warm
dry		

→ boiling hot; scorching hot

wet weather
damp	rainy

WEATHER WORDS: NOUNS

changeable weather
breeze	showers
rainbow	sunshine

hot weather
drought	heatwave	sun

stormy weather
blizzard	hail	storm
gale	lightning	thunder
gust	snowstorm	wind

wet weather
downpour	sleet
rain	wet

WEATHER WORDS: VERBS

wet weather
drizzle	pour	rain

→ bucket down; rain cats and dogs

weird ADJECTIVE

Something that is **weird** seems strange and peculiar.

curious

They were on the way to school when a curious thing happened.

extraordinary

Suddenly an extraordinary bird appeared in the garden.

funny

"That's funny," said Mum. "I made twelve cakes. Now there are only ten."

odd

They heard an odd creaking sound coming from the cellar, and looked at each other in alarm.

peculiar

The stone was covered in peculiar marks, like ancient writing.

strange

Today a strange notice appeared in the sweetshop window.

unusual

The woman was wearing an unusual hat.

→ spooky

wet (1) ADJECTIVE

If something is **wet**, it is covered in water or other liquid.

damp

The ground was damp, so they sat on a waterproof rug.

drenched

Holly was drenched by the time she got to school.

moist

Robin checked that the soil in the plant pot was moist.

soaked

Lizzie wished she'd worn boots. Her trainers were soaked.

→ like a drowned rat; soaked to the skin

ANTONYM: dry

wet (2) ADJECTIVE

If the weather is **wet**, it is raining.

drizzly

It was drizzly outside, but not worth taking an umbrella.

misty

The misty air left droplets of water on leaves and flowers.

rainy

It was a rainy Sunday afternoon, and Sanjay was bored.

showery

Julia's jacket was great for showery weather, although it was starting to get a bit small.

stormy

We only had one day of stormy weather before the canal flooded.

ANTONYM: dry or fine

wet (3) VERB

If you **wet** something, you put liquid on it.

dampen

Gran always dampens her washing before she irons it.

drown

The river burst its banks and drowned Anastasia's garden for the second time in a year.

soak

The ride at the theme park soaked Mum through to the skin.

spatter

The dog shook itself vigorously and spattered everybody.

splash

A passing car splashed Emily from head to foot.

water

Make sure you water the soil around the new plants.

ANTONYM: dry

a
b
c
d
e
f
g
h
i
j
k
l
m
n
o
p
q
r
s
t
u
v
Ww
x
y
z

wicked

wicked ADJECTIVE
Someone or something **wicked** is very bad.

evil
There is an **evil** witch in the story of Hansel and Gretel.

foul
"Who has done this **foul** deed?" cried the angry king.

vicious
He was a cruel and **vicious** man.

vile
Many **vile** things happen during a war.

wild (1) ADJECTIVE
Wild animals, birds and plants live in natural surroundings and are not looked after by people.

free
Many colourful birds fly **free** in rainforests.

natural
In the countryside, plants and insects live in **natural** conditions.

untamed
In some places, horses run **untamed**.

wild (2) ADJECTIVE
If the weather is **wild**, it is rough and stormy.

rough
The boat was tossed around on **rough** seas.

stormy
It was a **stormy** night and the lifeboat crew was ready for trouble.

violent
A **violent** storm swept the island.

wild (3) ADJECTIVE
Wild behaviour is not controlled.

boisterous
All the children became **boisterous** when their team won.

chaotic
Chaotic scenes greeted Mrs Jones when she came back into the room.

noisy
The class was so **noisy** the teacher couldn't make herself heard.

rough
Some of the games got a bit **rough**.

rowdy
My dad's strict and he won't put up with **rowdy** behaviour.

willing ADJECTIVE
If you are **willing** to do something, you are ready and happy to do it.

eager
William was **eager** to help wash the car.

happy
Emma said she'd be **happy** to get her grandmother's shopping.

prepared
Josh said he was **prepared** to do the washing-up for a week.

ready
Rob was always **ready** to take the dog for a walk.

ANTONYM: **unwilling**

win (1) VERB

If you **win** a race or game, you do better than the others taking part.

come first

*"Did you **come first**?" asked the coach.*

succeed

*Lisa entered the painting competition, determined to **succeed**.*

triumph

*Tweedledum was determined to **triumph** in the battle against his brother.*

ANTONYM: lose

win (2) VERB

If you **win** something such as a prize, you get it for doing something well.

earn

*Rachel was delighted to **earn** herself a place in the team.*

get

*Jeremy **got** a prize for swimming.*

receive

*Indigo **received** a cup for being Student of the Year.*

secure

*My brother finally **secured** a place in the football team.*

wind VERB

If a road or river **winds**, it has lots of bends in it.

curve

*Further along, the river **curves** round a steep bank.*

snake

*The road **snakes** to and fro along the edge of the cliff.*

turn

*In the middle of the wood the path suddenly **turns** off to the left.*

twist

*The lane **twists** dangerously here, so drivers have to be extra careful.*

wipe VERB

If you **wipe** something, you rub its surface lightly to remove dirt or liquid.

dry

*I quickly **dried** the table with a tissue to get rid of the spilt milk.*

dust

*There was no time to **dust** the sideboard before the visitors arrived.*

mop

*We had to **mop** the kitchen floor after we'd tramped through in our football boots.*

polish

*Dad **polished** his favourite shoes ready for the interview.*

rub

*"You'll have to **rub** a bit harder than that," said Mum.*

wise ADJECTIVE

If someone tells you it would be **wise** to do something, they mean it would be sensible.

intelligent

*I think the **intelligent** thing to do would be to go straight home.*

reasonable

*We thought it was **reasonable** at the time.*

sensible

*She couldn't decide what would be a **sensible** course of action.*

ANTONYM: foolish

wither

wither VERB

If a plant **withers**, it shrivels up and dies.

droop
*Dad rushed out to water the flowers because they were **drooping**.*

dry up
*All my seedlings **dried up** in the sun.*

shrink
*In the drought, the runner beans **shrank** to half their normal size.*

shrivel
*The leaves on the tree **shrivelled** instead of turning a glorious red.*

wilt
*She put the wrong food on the houseplant and it soon began to **wilt**.*

wobble VERB

If something **wobbles**, it makes small movements from side to side.

shake
*The table **shook** every time Dad tried to write his list of things to fix.*

tremble
*His knees **trembled** with fear.*

vibrate
*Whenever a lorry went past, everything on the shelf **vibrated**.*

work (1) VERB

When you **work**, you spend time and energy doing something useful.

labour
*Cinderella was expected to **labour** all day for the ugly sisters.*

slave
*The witch said she was tired of **slaving** over a hot cauldron.*

slog INFORMAL
*Emily always seemed to be **slogging** away at something or other.*

toil
*All day, Grandpa **toiled** in the hot sun.*

work (2) VERB

If something **works**, it does what it is supposed to do.

function
*Gus complained his computer wasn't **functioning** properly.*

go
*Esther shook her watch, trying to make it **go**.*

run
*The car **ran** well after the mechanic had mended it.*

work (3) NOUN

Work can be someone's job.

business
*His **business** is mainly buying and selling computers.*

career
*My sister's **career** as a pilot takes her all over the world.*

craft
*The **craft** that Uncle Freddy enjoys best is woodcarving.*

job
*Alison is hoping that her new **job** will be better paid.*

profession
*Doctor Collins says he feels his **profession** is worthwhile.*

trade
*Our plumber is proud of his **trade**.*

worry (1) VERB

If you **worry**, you keep thinking about problems or about unpleasant things that might happen.

be anxious
*You can tell that my brother **is anxious** about his piano exam.*

brood
*Surely you're not still **brooding** about what she said?*

feel uneasy
*She was **feeling uneasy** about making the journey on her own.*

fret
*Please stop **fretting**! You can't change anything now.*

worry (2) VERB

If you **worry** someone, you disturb them with a problem.

bother
*Don't **bother** me now. I'm just going out.*

hassle INFORMAL
*Your sister says you keep **hassling** her.*

pester
*I wish they'd stop **pestering** me.*

plague
*My brother said I should work it out for myself and not **plague** him with questions.*

trouble
*"I hate to **trouble** you," said Mum, "but shouldn't you be doing some homework?"*

wrong (1) ADJECTIVE

Something that is **wrong** is not correct.

false
*She couldn't decide if he gave a **false** answer on purpose.*

faulty
*The wiring on that iron is **faulty**. It could be dangerous.*

incorrect
*In general the story is true, but some of the details are **incorrect**.*

mistaken
*I'm sure you're **mistaken**. That couldn't have been Spencer.*

untrue
*Jasper's story about his dad being an astronaut was quite **untrue**.*

➜ wide of the mark

ANTONYM:

wrong (2) ADJECTIVE

If a person does something **wrong**, they do something bad.

bad
*The way the ugly sisters treated Cinderella was **bad**.*

crooked
*Using stolen credit cards is a **crooked** way to behave.*

dishonest
*Beth knew it was **dishonest** to ride on a train without paying.*

wicked
*It was **wicked** to give Snow White a poisoned apple.*

a
b
c
d
e
f
g
h
i
j
k
l
m
n
o
p
q
r
s
t
u
v
Ww
x
y
z

Xx Yy Zz

young (1)   ADJECTIVE

A **young** person, animal or plant has not been alive for very long.

adolescent
*Two **adolescent** boys ran to help the old lady when she fell.*

fresh
*Mum went to the vegetable garden to cut a **fresh** lettuce.*

immature
*My older sister can behave in a very **immature** way.*

infant
*Joshua just didn't want to play with his **infant** friends.*

junior
*The youth club has plenty of things for **junior** members to do.*

little
*Outside the shop a **little** boy was crying. He said he was lost.*

teenage
*Holly scanned the library shelves for **teenage** fiction.*

unfledged
*Mary found an **unfledged** bird on the ground. It had fallen from its nest.*

youthful
*My dad must be quite old, although he still looks **youthful**.*

ANTONYM: old

young (2)   PLURAL NOUN

The **young** of an animal are its babies.

brood
*The mother hen gathered her **brood** under her wings.*

family
*Our cat has four new kittens and is very proud of her **family**.*

litter
*Star's **litter** occupied the whole basket and some of the kitchen floor.*

offspring
*Female animals are usually very protective of their **offspring**.*

YOUNG ANIMALS:
A young bear is a cub.
A young cat is a kitten.
A young chicken is a chick.
A young cow is a calf.
A young deer is a fawn.
A young dog is a puppy.
A young duck is a duckling.
A young elephant is a calf.
A young fox is a cub.
A young goat is a kid.
A young goose is a gosling.
A young hare is a leveret.
A young horse is a foal.
A young kangaroo is a joey.
A young lion is a cub.
A young pig is a piglet.
A young rabbit is a kitten.
A young seal is a calf or pup.
A young sheep is a lamb.
A young swan is a cygnet.
A young tiger is a cub.
A young whale is a calf.
A young wolf is a cub.

SOME MOTHERS AND YOUNG:

bear and cub

cat and kitten

deer and fawn

horse and foal

kangaroo and joey

goat and kid

pig and piglet

rabbit and kitten

tiger and cub

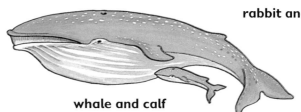
whale and calf

zero NOUN

You can use **zero** to mean none at all.

nil
*They knew their chances of Dad taking them to the cinema were **nil** unless they promised to behave.*

none at all
*Old Mother Hubbard looked for food in her cupboard, but there was **none at all**.*

nothing
*There was **nothing** Jackie could find to wear for the evening out.*

zigzag VERB

If something **zigzags**, it goes in a line that keeps changing direction sharply.

bend
*Rory tried to draw a straight line, but it **bent** all over the place.*

twist
*The road **twisted** dangerously and Dad found it hard to control the car.*

wind
*A narrow track **wound** across the field. It was made by sheep and goats.*

A–Z Index

See 'Using the index' for instructions on how to use this synonym index.

Bb

cackle

Cc

cackle . . . . **laugh** 95
cake . . . . **lump** 99
calamity . . . . **accident** 8
calculate . . . . **count** 33
call . . . . **cry** 35
call . . . . **shout** 140
calm . . . . **gentle** 64
calm . . . . **peace** 115
calm . . . . **quiet** 125
camouflage . . . . . **disguise** 40
can of worms . . . . **problem** 121
cap . . . . **top** 170
capacity . . . . **space** 148
caper . . . . **skip** 142
capture . . . . **catch** 25
care . . . . **mind** 105
care for . . . . **keep** 92
careless . . . . **bad** 12
career . . . . **work** 188
caring . . . . **good** 67
caring . . . . **helpful** 78
caring . . . . **thoughtful** 166
carry . . . . **bring** 21
carry . . . . **hold** 80
carry . . . . **move** 107
carry . . . . **take** 160
carry on . . . . . . **keep** 92
carry on . . . . . . **last** 95
carry out . . . . . . **do** 40
carton . . . . **box** 20
cartoon . . . . **picture** 116
carve . . . . **cut** 35
cascade . . . . **flow** 55

case . . . . **box** 20
cast around . . . . . **search** 134
casual . . . . **informal** 86
catastrophe . . . . . **accident** 8
catch fire . . . . . . **light** 97
catch sight of . . . . **spot** 151
cautious . . . . **careful** 25
cautious . . . . **shy** 142
cave . . . . **hole** 80
celebrated . . . . . . **great** 69
cement . . . . **glue** 66
centre . . . . **middle** 104
certain . . . . **sure** 158
challenge . . . . . . **play** 119
championship . . . . **competition** 31
chance . . . . **accident** 8
chance . . . . **turn** 174
change into . . . . . **turn into** 175
changed . . . . **different** 38
chaos . . . . **mess** 104
chaotic . . . . **wild** 186
charming . . . . . . **attractive** 11
charming . . . . . . **pleasant** 119
chase . . . . **follow** 57
chat . . . . **conversation** . . . 31
chat . . . . **talk** 161
cheat . . . . **trick** 172
check . . . . **test** 164
check out . . . . . . **try** 174
cheer . . . . **encourage** 46
cheerful . . . . . . **bright** 21
cheerful . . . . . . **happy** 75
cheerful . . . . . . **pleasant** 119
cheerful . . . . . . **warm** 181
chest . . . . **box** 20

collect

crevice

Ee

flimsy	**light**	97
flimsy	**thin**	165
flimsy	**weak**	183
fling	**move**	107
fling	**scatter**	133
fling	**throw**	166
flock	**gather**	63
flood	**flow**	55
flourish	**grow**	72
flourish	**shake**	137
flowing	**graceful**	68
fluffy	**soft**	145
fluid	**juice**	91
flutter	**fly**	57
fly	**hurry**	82
fly	**move**	107
foam	**boil**	19
fold	**bend**	15
follow	**chase**	26
follow	**copy**	32
follow	**see**	135
follow	**understand**	176
fool	**trick**	172
foolish	**silly**	142
foolish	**stupid**	157
foot	**bottom**	19
forbid	**ban**	13
force	**drive**	43
force	**effort**	45
force	**make**	100
force	**power**	121
force	**push**	123
force	**thrust**	167
foreign	**strange**	155
forged	**false**	50
forgery	**copy**	32
forlorn	**lonely**	98
form	**make**	100
form	**shape**	138
foul	**dirty**	39
foul	**wicked**	186
foundation	**bottom**	19
fountain	**jet**	88
fragile	**weak**	183
fragment	**bit**	17
fragment	**part**	114
fragrance	**smell**	144
frail	**fragile**	58
frail	**weak**	183
free	**save**	131
free	**wild**	186
freezing	**cold**	29
frequently	**often**	112
fresh	**young**	190
fret	**worry**	189
friendless	**lonely**	98
friendly	**helpful**	78
friendly	**informal**	86
friendly	**kind**	93
friendly	**nice**	110
friendly	**pleasant**	119
friendly	**warm**	181
fright	**fear**	52
frighten	**bully**	23
frighten	**disturb**	40
frighten	**scare**	133
frightening	**dreadful**	42
frightful	**dreadful**	42
frisky	**lively**	97
frosty	**cold**	29

Hh

Ii

Jj

Kk

Ll

Mm

mean	**horrible**	81
mean	**nasty**	110
means	**way**	183
meek	**mild**	105
meet	**gather**	63
meet	**join**	90
meet	**touch**	170
menacing	**dangerous**	37
mend	**fix**	55
mention	**tell**	163
merciless	**harsh**	76
messy	**careless**	25
messy	**dirty**	39
method	**plan**	118
method	**way**	183
microscopic	**invisible**	87
microscopic	**tiny**	169
midpoint	**middle**	104
might	**force**	58
mighty	**big**	16
mighty	**strong**	156
migrate	**move**	107
mimic	**copy**	32
mind	**care**	24
mind	**watch**	181
mind-numbing	**boring**	19
mingle	**mix**	106
miniature	**tiny**	169
minute	**small**	144
minute	**tiny**	169
mirror	**copy**	32
miserable	**dull**	43
miserable	**sad**	130
miserable	**unhappy**	176
miserly	**mean**	102

misery	**grief**	70
mishap	**accident**	8
mistaken	**wrong**	189
misty	**wet**	185
mixed	**different**	38
mixture	**variety**	178
mob	**group**	70
modest	**plain**	118
modest	**shy**	142
modify	**change**	26
moist	**wet**	185
momentary	**short**	140
monotonous	**boring**	19
mop	**wipe**	187
mop up	**clean**	27
morsel	**bit**	17
morsel	**taste**	162
mosaic	**picture**	116
mound	**heap**	77
mound	**pile**	117
mountain	**pile**	117
mouthwatering	**delicious**	37
move	**carry**	25
move house	**move**	107
mow	**cut**	35
muggy	**stuffy**	157
multiply	**grow**	72
multiply	**increase**	85
munch	**eat**	44
mural	**picture**	116
murder	**kill**	92
murky	**dark**	37
murmur	**say**	132
mystifying	**mysterious**	109
mystifying	**strange**	155

Nn

Oo

Pp

Qq

Rr

remote

travel

Uu